THE ORGANIST AND CHOIRMASTER

BY Charles L. Etherington

THE MACMILLAN COMPANY
New York · 1952

First Printing

PRINTED IN THE UNITED STATES OF AMERICA

Acknowledgements

¶ The pointing of the first four verses of the Magnificat, on pages 48 and 49, is reprinted from THE OXFORD PSALTER by permission of the Oxford University Press.

¶ The examples of pointing on pages 39 to 45 are from THE CATHEDRAL PSALTER, and the portion of Psalm XXVII on pages 49 to 51 is from THE ENGLISH PSALTER. These examples, and references to THE CATHEDRAL PRAYER BOOK, are used by permission of Novello & Company, Limited.

To the Very Reverend

HOWARD H. CLARK,

Dean of Ottawa

PREFACE

This book is not intended for experienced Anglican organists and choirmasters, who are already in possession of the information contained within its covers.

It is hoped that it may serve as a guide to church musicians who, unfamiliar with Anglican services and traditions, find themselves called upon to prepare music for the services of that church. It often happens that an organist and choirmaster of recognized ability, upon taking service, or desiring to take service in an Anglican church, is bewildered by the ritual and forms with which he has never had an opportunity of becoming acquainted.

And, more particularly, these pages are designed for the assistance of organists and choirmasters in smaller communities. Too often, our village and country churches (and there are thousands of them) find it necessary to engage the services of any musician who happens to be available, whatever his ability or experience. If he is not an Anglican, he is sorely in need of instruction: even if he is conversant with the services, he may know no other standard than that established in his own parish by a line of indifferent or uninformed predecessors. He may have few or no opportunities of hearing and observing services in other Anglican churches, and so lack the advantage of comparing his own work and methods with those of more experienced colleagues. Because of a necessarily limited outlook, he may fail to raise the music of his parish church to the highest possible standard.

For such there is, as far as I know, no written work to serve as a manual. The Prayer Book itself, while setting forth the services to be used, offers little advice as to how they are to be conducted;

the many psalters and service books available may easily confuse the uninitiated by their diversity. This book has been written in an attempt to overcome this lack—to inform, stimulate and encourage the thousands of organists and choirmasters upon whom the church relies for the preservation of its heritage of church music.

This manual would fail in its purpose if it left in the mind of the reader the impression that an attempt was being made to set forth a rigid, unalterable formula for the music of the church. Each parish has its own local customs and traditions: in some places the services are plain, mostly said; in others, music is used wherever possible. The organist is advised to respect local usage, and to avoid sudden or drastic changes which might upset the congregation. For the intelligent preparation of his work, however, he should be familiar with the traditions and trends of church music, and the general broad principles followed by Anglican cathedral choirs for centuries.

In order that the work may prove useful to the several branches of the Anglican communion, references are made to the Books of Common Prayer of the Church of England, the Church of England in Canada, and the Protestant Episcopal Church of the United States of America. In the interests of brevity, these are referred to as the English, Canadian and American books respectively.

Throughout the book, the term "rector" is rather loosely used to denote the minister, whether he is actually a rector, a vicar, or a priest-in-charge. This is the general practice in Canada and the United States, although in England the distinction is more strictly observed.

CHARLES L. ETHERINGTON

Fergus, Ontario,
February, 1952.

Contents

I · THE SERVANTS OF THE CHURCH *page 1*

§ 1 The Choirmaster *1*
§ 2 The Organist *5*
§ 3 The Choristers *8*

II · THE SEASONS OF THE CHURCH *12*

§ 1 Calendars and Lectionaries *12*
§ 2 Advent *13*
§ 3 Christmas-tide *15*
§ 4 Epiphany-tide *17*
§ 5 "Little Lent" *17*
§ 6 Lent *19*
§ 7 Easter-tide *20*
§ 8 Ascension-tide *22*
§ 9 Whitsun-tide *22*
§ 10 The Trinity Season *23*
§ 11 Saints' Days and Other Holy Days *23*
§ 12 Black Letter Days *27*
§ 13 Special Services *27*
§ 14 National Observances *28*

CHURCH CALENDAR *29*

III · THE MUSIC OF THE CHURCH *37*

§ 1 The Canticles and Psalms *37*
§ 2 The Versicles and Responses *54*
§ 3 The Hymns *58*
§ 4 Anthems *68*
§ 5 Organ Music *71*
§ 6 Education in Church Music *74*

IV · THE SERVICES OF THE CHURCH *79*

§ 1 General Notes *79*
§ 2 Morning Prayer *80*
§ 3 Evening Prayer *100*
§ 4 The Litany *102*
§ 5 The Communion Service *105*
§ 6 Publick Baptism of Infants *or* Holy Baptism *121*
§ 7 The Order of Confirmation *123*
§ 8 The Solemnization of Matrimony *124*
§ 9 The Burial of the Dead *127*
§ 10 Commination Service *or* Penitential Office *129*
§ 11 Accession Service *130*
§ 12 Dominion Day Service *131*
§ 13 Children's Service *132*
§ 14 Service for Missions *132*
§ 15 Harvest Thanksgiving *133*
§ 16 Institution and Induction of Ministers *134*
§ 17 Laying of a Foundation Stone *138*
§ 18 Consecration of a Church or Chapel *139*
§ 19 Organ Recitals and Other Musical Services *141*

V · EQUIPMENT AND ORGANIZATION *144*

§ 1 The Organ *144*
§ 2 The Choir Stalls *152*
§ 3 Vestments *153*
§ 4 Books *156*
§ 5 Service Lists *158*
§ 6 The Choir Vestry *162*
§ 7 The Practice Room *163*

§ 8 Finances 164
§ 9 Organization 165

VI · CHOIR ETIQUETTE 169

CONCLUSION 173

INDEX 174

I · THE SERVANTS OF THE CHURCH

§1 The Choirmaster

The rector of the parish is, strictly speaking, responsible for the music as he is responsible for every other detail of the service. However, except in the occasional country church where no capable person is available, the responsibility for the music is generally delegated to someone engaged for that purpose.

It is the duty of the choirmaster to select and prepare the music of the church; and to choose, train, and maintain discipline among his choristers.

Perhaps the majority of clergymen choose the hymns and psalms, and decide upon the canticles to be used at the services. A few of them designate the tunes, but that decision rests properly with the choirmaster. Very often the rector will leave the choice of hymns and psalms to a choirmaster in whose ability and good judgement he has confidence.

The privilege of exercising a free hand in the music of the church is not easily earned, for the successful preparation of an Anglican service requires more than musical ability. Musicians of good reputation, with fine organs and trained choirs at their disposal, have often proved disappointing in the Anglican church because of their unfamiliarity with the background and traditions of the services.

On the other hand, one occasionally hears a service inspiringly played and sung by an organist and choir of limited musical ability, but with an intimate knowledge of Anglican usage, and the good sense to confine their efforts to music within their limitations.

The choirmaster, then, should be thoroughly familiar with the services, seasons, rituals and traditions of the church at large; and, of course, fully cognizant of any variations and peculiarities which obtain in his particular parish. He should be able, after consultation with his rector, to plan in such a way that each service will be a continuous whole—hymns, psalms, anthems, lessons and sermon combining to impress upon the people the message of the church's season or the subject chosen by the rector. Such a well-planned service is infinitely more effective than a hodge-podge of hymns, psalms, etc. which are not closely related to one another or to the lessons and sermon.

In his work, the choirmaster will come into contact chiefly with the clergy and the choir.

As has been said, the rector is the authority where the services are concerned, and the choirmaster should do his best to carry out his rector's wishes. Most clergymen are glad to have frequent consultations with their choirmasters, and will respect the judgement of one who is capable, hard-working and zealous. They do not, as a rule, adopt a sympathetic attitude towards church musicians who are seeking prominence and personal glory before the good of the church, and one can scarcely blame them for that. Generally speaking, a choirmaster whose chief aim is to make the services beautiful and devotional will find in his rector a warm friend and a staunch ally.

There are a few clergymen who pretend no interest in the music of the church. Their choirmasters are at a disadvantage in not being able to discuss their plans with their rectors; but even in such cases it is possible, by care and alertness, to prepare satisfactory services.

Occasionally (one must be frank!) a choirmaster will become associated with a rector who interferes in the music to such an extent that the choirmaster becomes a nonentity. Unfortunately, the rare clergymen who thus interfere have, as a rule, no knowledge of music or of the problems which the choirmaster has to solve. In such a situation, the choirmaster would be well advised to seek service elsewhere. Conflict is as useless as it is unseemly for, whatever the merits of the case, the rector remains the authority.

Contact with other clergy of the parish (if there are others) is generally unofficial. The choirmaster may be required to instruct a new curate in the manner of intoning the service in his parish, and he will do well to discuss preparations for the service with a curate who is to preach.

The choirmaster's association with the lay officials of the church —chiefly the wardens—is usually confined to financial matters: salary, supplies for the choir, the care of the organ, etc. Some churches have an elected body called the Select Vestry, but any opinions they may desire to express concerning the music are properly conveyed to the choirmaster through the wardens or, better still, through the rector.

Music committees are not the rule in the Anglican church, but they are sometimes encountered. They are of three kinds: those that confine their duties to arranging for the tuning and maintenance of the organ, the supplying of books and anthems, and the provision of vestments, may be of real assistance in relieving the choirmaster of responsibilities that should not be his; those which do nothing can be tolerated; but those who seek to justify their appointment by interfering in the music of the church and the personnel of the choir are nothing more than nuisances.

Choirmasters should not expect to become laws unto themselves, but they should be considered competent of performing the duties allotted to them. The interests of the church are best served when instructions regarding the services are given only by the rector. All church musicians receive suggestions, some helpful, some foolish. The wise man listens courteously, and considers those suggestions that promise to be of benefit.

The Anglican choirmaster's associations with his choir are exactly the same as those of a choirmaster in any other church. The ability to exert authority and maintain discipline, while retaining the friendship and respect of his choristers, is a matter of personality and temperament rather than the subject of a book. It is not always easy to reconcile the needs of the choir with the convenience of the choristers; but the man who sets an example of enthusiasm and hard work, and who treats his choristers with courtesy and consideration, is not likely to have much trouble.

But much of the choirmaster's work is done alone, in study and preparation. He should be able to choose his material intelligently, having regard both to its appropriateness for the service under consideration, and to its practicability from the standpoint of the choir. This duty requires not only a certain knowledge (of which it is hoped that this book may impart a little) but a willingness to devote some time to the matter. A hasty choosing of hymns and chants an hour or two before rehearsal time will usually have unsatisfactory results.

Time should be taken not only for the selection of the music, but for its study. The choirmaster should make himself familiar with the words of the hymns, psalms and anthems he intends to use; he must decide the phrasing, and know what passages are likely to give his choir trouble; he should know each part as thoroughly as he hopes his singers will know it. This familiarity is not acquired by a cursory glance.

Unless he is to remain in a rut, the choirmaster should examine new music, and older music with which he is not familiar. Most publishers are glad to supply music "on approval" and to keep the choirmaster informed as to the newer trends in church music.

It is wise also to examine new psalters and service books in these days when the whole system of chanting is undergoing a change.

Finally, the choirmaster should strive to submerge personal ambition and to avoid showmanship. The most carefully prepared service can be marred by a conductor who, by exaggerated gestures, attracts the attention of the congregation towards himself. There is a general misconception that humility leads to weak submission and obscurity. True humility goes hand in hand with quiet dignity, and earns more respect than any amount of showmanship. In church music, as in any other activity, a great deal of noise and the desire for prominence may bring satisfaction for a time; but it is the man who performs his duties conscientiously, earnestly and competently who wins the lasting regard of those with whom he is associated.

§2 The Organist

The organist (who is generally also the choirmaster) should, of course, strive constantly to improve his work by study and practice.

One can scarcely imagine an organist—student or veteran—coming to a service without some preparation, but too many organists are much better prepared for their voluntaries and postludes than for their duties as accompanists. No sensible person would advise a student to neglect his technical studies and organ literature (no sensible student would heed such advice!) but he who undertakes the playing of a church service must realize that his principal role is that of accompanist, and that if he fails in that role he fails completely in the judgement of his congregation, play he Bach fugues ever so expertly.

From a purely technical point of view, the playing of hymn tunes is a fairly simple matter. Yet, of two organists playing the same chords with the same degree of accuracy, one may infuse the service with life and warmth, while the other may be uninspiring to the point of dreariness. The difference between the two is not accidental: it is not always a matter of talent, either, for a brilliant recitalist may prove to be a broken reed when the clergy, choir and congregation are looking to him for support and inspiration. It is a matter of forethought and attention to detail.

The singing of hymns by a congregation of untrained voices requires a great deal of inspiration and suggestion from the organ if it is to have much meaning. We all deplore the sentimental fellow who keeps one foot on the expression pedal and pumps it in and out with little or no provocation; but there are many opportunities of emphasizing the sentiment of the words without making one's accompaniment spectacular or ridiculous. It might be observed that such emphasis is not always achieved by increasing or decreasing volume: a change of registration may be even more effective than adding stronger stops or opening the swell box. The point is that the organist should devote part of his study period to becoming familiar with the hymns and finding out what sort of accompaniment aids best in deepening and strengthening the sentiment of the words. The too confident player who scorns the practising of hymn tunes will, despite all the presence of mind he may possess, miss many opportunities for effective playing.

The accompaniment for the canticles and psalms is likely to require more preparation than the hymns. The organist should be well versed in the general principles of chanting and, particularly, in the method used in his church.

It is prudent to memorize either the words or the chant, for the necessity of shifting one's eyes from chant to words and back again may result in losing one's place. The pointing of frequently used canticles and psalms will soon become familiar; but when playing without reference to the printed page, one should rely on *memory* rather than *habit* which may prove treacherous at times.

Strange things have been known to happen during the singing of psalms and, while the organist should not be considered a crutch for a weak choir to lean upon, he should be well enough prepared to take command of the situation if confusion threatens.

Accompaniments for anthems are often ill-prepared. When the organ merely duplicates the voice parts, little preparation is necessary; but when the organ part is more or less independent of the voices, care should be taken that it is given enough yet not too much prominence. Many lovely passages upon which composers have lavished thought and skill are entirely lost to the congregation because the organist has not thought it worth while to devise a suitable registration. The choir cannot make the anthem a work of art if the accompaniment is slovenly.

In accompanying a small choir whose range of volume is necessarily smaller than that of a large group of singers, the careful organist can do much to heighten contrasts by using the facilities for expression that his instrument provides.

In addition to the usual accomplishments (the preparation of pieces and accompaniments for the choir) the Anglican organist should be fairly adept at improvisation and modulation.

There are many places in the service where a few chords are required to avoid "dead spots"—when the people are rising from their knees after prayers, or when the sidesmen are returning to their pews after the presentation of the alms. Only the organist can fill these brief gaps, and then only if he can improvise at least a little.

The necessity of passing from one part of the service to another without interruption, and without abrupt and unpleasant changes of key requires some proficiency in modulation. The organist who has not yet acquired the skill may find some aid in sets of ready-made modulations and interludes which may be obtained from music publishers. However, a good ear, a not too profound knowledge of harmony, and constant practice will result in some degree of proficiency which will give the organist far more satisfaction than he can derive from the printed page.

It might be argued that anyone who cannot improvise and modulate should not be playing a church organ. There are, in small communities, countless men and women of limited ability who are keeping church music alive, either because more experienced people are not available, or because professional musicians scorn to serve for the trifling remuneration that is offered by some small churches. These valiant souls deserve more encouragement and respect than they usually receive; and, in view of the handicaps under which they work, they often accomplish more than their more fortunate brethren in large and splendidly equipped city churches. However, while their shortcomings may be overlooked because of their devotion, there is no excuse for neglect of self-improvement on their part.

The organist, whether he is the choirmaster or not, should be thoroughly familiar with the Prayer Book and the services. It goes without saying that he will cultivate a good taste in organ music, for the selection of pieces is in his hands even when the direction of choral music is the responsibility of another.

§3 The Choristers

The choristers of an Anglican church are on duty oftener than singers of most other churches. They must expect to be present for services on Christmas Day, Ash Wednesday, Good Friday, Ascension Day, and perhaps at other services besides those of Sundays. Furthermore, they must be regular in attendance at rehearsals, for in most Anglican churches at least part of the service is always sung whether there is to be any "special" music or not. Even an experienced choir becomes slovenly unless the sung parts of the service are practised at frequent intervals.

Perhaps the first qualification for a choir prospect, then, after an ability to sing or some promise of becoming a singer, is reliability.

There is an unhappy tendency towards "big" choirs whether they are efficient or not; and in some churches, both the rector and the choirmaster are more concerned about adding members to the choir than they are about the quality of the music. Excellent work can be done with a small, interested group: no progress at all can be made with a choir, large or small, whose members are irregular in attendance.

In considering a candidate for the choir, it is well to make some quiet inquiries concerning him. If he is an habitual "joiner" who holds membership in several organizations and is loyal to none, he will probably be of no assistance to the choir. He will neglect services and practices for anything else that turns up.

Admittedly, people who can be relied upon to place their duty to the choir before other considerations are few; and when the choir is small, there is a temptation to relax the attendance rules in order to obtain the occasional services of a good singer. It is unwise to do so. It is unfair to the reliable choristers to tolerate members who are irregular; and the crowning insult is to postpone the singing of an anthem, which has been practised diligently by the majority of the choir, because two or three irresponsible ones have been absent from rehearsal.

One other important qualification for a chorister is the willingness to sink his own personality—to regard himself as a part of the whole choir rather than as an individual. The Anglican church choir is no place for the "star soloist." Indeed, solos are not the general rule except when they occur in anthems, and even then the soloist sings as a voice in the choir.

One of the most important duties of a choirmaster is the careful planning of rehearsals. The choir should be kept busy to avoid talking and inattention. Variety and some new music aid in maintaining interest.

In fairness to his choristers (as well as to the church and to himself) the choirmaster should put new music into practice far enough in advance to insure a good performance. Choristers should not be asked to sing anything that they do not know thoroughly; and they can learn their parts thoroughly only if ample time is allowed for rehearsal. In some cases it may be advisable to begin practising Christmas music as early as October, Easter music soon after the Epiphany, and Harvest Festival anthems before the summer vacation. By so spreading out the work, routine music from Sunday to Sunday need not be neglected, and the festival music is well prepared. It is much better to have festival music ready two or three weeks before it is required than to find it necessary to call extra last-minute rehearsals which are more likely to upset than reassure those concerned. This policy of preparedness should be extended to everything that is sung by the choir in order that they may always perform their duties with confidence (although not with complacency, of course)!

In smaller places where voices are untrained, knowledge of music slight, and singers hard to obtain, the choirmaster will require a tremendous amount of patience, courage, ambition and determination. Yet it is astonishing what can be done with unpromising material by a man who resolves to make the most of and improve his resources. The choirmaster should never adopt, or allow his choristers to adopt the attitude that "ours is only a village choir, after all, and not much can be expected of us." The ultimate objective of every choir should be a cathedral choir standard; and, while that objective may never be reached, the striving for it will result in noticeable improvement.

Fortunately, much good church music is simple. Anthems and services in unison and in two or three parts are available for choirs which do not include four parts. It is well to choose music to suit the capabilities of one's choir, postponing the introduction of more ambitious music until such time as the choir is prepared for it.

Sometimes men with good voices are unable to read music. It is a good policy to divide such men into small groups and train them in sight-singing. The ability to sing the tenor or bass of a few hymn tunes will give them a great deal of confidence and satisfaction, and their development will be a grand experience for the man who trains them.

The inclusion of boys in the choir is traditional in the Anglican church, and the choirmaster whose soprano section does not consist partly or wholly of boys is neglecting his opportunities. In a small choir of from twelve to twenty members, even four or five boys will add much. They learn quickly, as a rule, and, in a choir where four parts are not available, they lend variety and beauty to the music by the singing of descants. Whether or not boys only are used in the soprano section depends upon the preference of the choirmaster and the material available.

In smaller parishes, the choirmaster cannot afford to be too particular about his voices, and he will sometimes make excellent choristers of boys whom the cathedral choirmaster would have rejected as beneath his notice. It must not be imagined, however, that one need only invite in lads from the street or from the Sunday School in order to have a boy soprano section. Nature endows most young boys with good voices, but the ability to use those voices must be acquired and cultivated if they are to be of any value.

There are many good books on the subject of training boys' voices, and there is no reason why lads in a little parish church should not have as good training and contribute as much to the service of the church as boys in a cathedral choir.

By starting in a modest way, overlooking no opportunities to add to his resources, and working out a well-defined, progressive programme, the right sort of man can raise the standard of music in a small church to a degree that was previously undreamed of. True, he will have to work harder than his colleagues in larger parishes, but he will be rewarded with more thrills and satisfaction. Only by putting his very best into the work, and by seeing that his choristers are rewarded with pleasure and some training can he expect his choir to be loyal and faithful servants of the church.

II · THE SEASONS OF THE CHURCH

§1 Calendars and Lectionaries

Familiarity with the seasons of the church year is a requisite of any Anglican organist and choirmaster. Each season—indeed, each Sunday and Holy Day—has its own particular theme which is set forth in the lessons, collect, epistle and gospel. The choirmaster (or clergyman) whose duty it is to choose hymns and anthems should consult the lectionary, collects, epistles and gospels very carefully in order that the sung parts of the service may conform to the traditional pattern of the church, and that the subject matter may coincide with that of the scriptural readings.

The church seasons are set out in order in the tables of lessons which are to be found in all Prayer Books immediately following the prefaces and some short, general directions regarding ceremonies and the reading of the Holy Scripture.

In the English book, the table headed *Lessons Proper for Sundays* sets out only one of the lessons for most Sundays of the year, although there are exceptions where both lessons are given. Immediately following is a table headed *Lessons Proper for Holy Days* which provides for festivals having fixed dates. The lessons not provided for in these tables, and for week days, are found a page or two farther on in *The Calendar with the Table of Lessons*, arranged according to the days of the month.

The Table of Lessons in the Canadian book, and *Psalms and Lessons for the Christian Year* in the American book provide complete sets of lessons for all Sundays and week days, arranged according to the church calendar.

Since the tables of lessons have been carefully planned with a definite object in mind, they are generally adhered to; but occasionally a clergyman may make use of some other lectionary, in which case the choirmaster should be provided with a copy. The choirmaster should also learn the rector's policy in regard to alternative lessons as set forth in the lectionary.

The Collects, Epistles and Gospels, which should be examined in conjunction with the lectionaries, may be found by consulting the tables of contents in the Prayer Books.

§2 Advent

The first season of the church year is Advent, which begins on the fourth Sunday before Christmas. (Any Sunday which occurs from November 27 to December 3 inclusive is the First Sunday in Advent.)

During Advent, the church reviews the Old Testament prophecies concerning the coming of the Messiah, repeats the gospel narratives of the events leading to the birth of Christ and the preaching of John the Baptist, and exhorts the people to repentance and preparation for the Second Coming of our Lord.

A safe guide to the selection of hymns will be found in the section of the hymnal headed "Advent"; but examination of the Scripture readings will often enable one to choose hymns which are particularly appropriate for certain Sundays in Advent.

The Second Sunday in Advent, often called "Bible Sunday," takes its main theme from the collect and epistle of the day, and is devoted chiefly to the Holy Scriptures. Hymns and anthems which have reference to the Word of God or to the spreading of the gospel are suitable.

The collect for any Sunday may be said at the evening service on the preceding Saturday; and the collect, epistle and gospel are used throughout the following week except on days for which a collect, epistle and gospel are appointed. Usually there is only one collect for each Sunday; but after the collect for the First Sunday in Advent there is a rubric ("rubric" is the term applied to the italicized directions which are printed throughout the Prayer Books) to the effect that it is to be used until Christmas Eve ("until Christmas Day" in the American book). Therefore, from the Second Sunday in Advent until Christmas two collects are read: that for the Second, Third or Fourth Sunday in Advent, followed by that of the First Sunday in Advent. This is an important point for organists to remember.

Also to be observed during the Advent season are three Ember Days—the Wednesday, Friday and Saturday after December 13, and always occurring in the week following the Third Sunday in Advent.

Ember Days are set apart for intercessions for the clergy, ordination candidates, and church workers in general. Hymns and anthems should mention the preaching of the gospel, the commissioning of apostles, teachers, etc. Some ordination hymns are appropriate.

The English Prayer Book contains no collect, epistle, gospel or proper lessons for Ember Days, but provision is made for them in the Canadian and American books.

In the Canadian book, the general *Table of Lessons* allows no interruption in the continuity of the readings which are begun on Advent Sunday. A few pages farther on, however, the table of *Lessons Proper for Special Days* does list appropriate lessons for these Ember Days in December, and these may well be consulted when hymns are being selected.

The American book appoints proper lessons in the table of *Psalms and Lessons for the Christian Year.*

Both the Canadian and American books contain a collect, epistle and gospel to be used on Ember Days. The collect will be followed by the collect for the First Sunday in Advent, and perhaps by that of the Third Sunday in Advent as well.

In churches where no services are held on Ember Days, the rector may decide to read the collect on the preceding or the following Sunday, in which case a suitable hymn may also be used.

§3 Christmas-tide

Of Christmas Day little need be said, for anyone not familiar with the spirit and the music of Christmas would scarcely be in the service of the Christian church or, indeed, a dweller in a Christian land. It might be mentioned, however, that in the Anglican church no Christmas music is used before the festival; the Sunday preceding is the Fourth Sunday in Advent, and should be observed as such. Seasonal music is reserved for Christmas Day and the week following.

In many churches a late service is held on Christmas Eve, in which case the collect, epistle and gospel are those of Christmas Day, and festival music is in order.

A carol service before Christmas is not inappropriate providing it is not sung until the last service for the Fourth Sunday in Advent has been held.

During the Christmas season occur three Holy Days; St. Stephen's Day (December 26), St. John the Evangelist's Day (December 27), and the Holy Innocents' Day (December 28). A consideration of these festivals belongs properly to a later section devoted to Holy Days; but, since the Prayer Books place their collects, epistles and gospels immediately after those for Christmas Day, and the same arrangement is followed in the Canadian and American lectionaries, it may be more convenient to mention them here.

In churches where services are not held daily, the feasts of St. Stephen, St. John the Evangelist and the Holy Innocents are often neglected in the festivities of Christmas. In the Canadian church, any of these festivals occurring on the First Sunday after Christmas is not observed: in the American church the saint's day takes precedence. (The English book contains no rules of precedence.) In any case, it is not unusual to have a hymn and the collect for the Holy Day on the Sunday after Christmas.

Some hymnals contain a hymn with opening and closing stanzas of a general saint's day character, with stanzas for each Holy Day which may be inserted as required. By using the stanzas for St.

Stephen, St. John and the Holy Innocents, this one hymn will serve to bring to mind all three Holy Days if no further observance is planned. Or any hymn commemorating the saints may be used, providing that hymns for apostles and evangelists are not used for St. Stephen and the Holy Innocents, and reference to martyrs is avoided on St. John's Day.

Where services are held daily, each Holy Day may be properly observed, its collect being followed by that of Christmas Day.

One other Holy Day falls in the Christmas season: the feast of the Circumcision of Christ on January 1. Music celebrating that event and making reference to the Name of Jesus is appropriate. Since this festival falls upon New Year's Day, hymns which mark the beginning of the year may be used.

In many churches a late service (sometimes called a Watch-Night service) is held on New Year's Eve, and the proper collect, epistle and gospel are those of the Circumcision.

The calendar provides for two Sundays after Christmas. If Christmas falls upon a Sunday, the following Sunday will be the feast of the Circumcision, and the collect, epistle, gospel and lessons for the First Sunday after Christmas will not be used. If Christmas falls upon a week day, however, the following Sunday will be observed as the First Sunday after Christmas (unless, in the American church, it be one of the feasts of St. Stephen, St. John the Evangelist, or the Holy Innocents), and the singing of festival music will be continued.

If a Sunday intervenes between the feasts of the Circumcision (January 1) and the Epiphany (January 6), it is observed as the Second Sunday after Christmas. All Prayer Books provide lessons for the Second Sunday after Christmas, but only the American book contains a collect, epistle and gospel. In the English and Canadian churches, the collect, epistle and gospel for the Circumcision are repeated. The hymns should refer to the nativity, circumcision and childhood of Jesus (some helpful material may be found among the Hymns for Children). Hymns suitable for the beginning of a new year may well be used.

§4 Epiphany-tide

The Feast of the Epiphany (January 6) commemorates the visit of the Wise Men to Bethlehem.

The entire Epiphany season deals with the manifestations of Christ during His life on earth. The Old Testament lessons are passages foretelling Christ's coming and the blessings resulting therefrom; the gospels and lessons from the evangelists tell of John the Baptist's preaching concerning Christ, of Christ's boyhood visit to the temple, of His baptism, of His appearance at the synagogue at Nazareth and to the Samaritans, and other occasions on which He made known His divine powers.

Suitable hymns will be found in the section of the hymnal devoted to the season, but the careful choirmaster will select words that apply particularly to that phase of Christ's earthly life which is given prominence in the gospel and lessons. Missionary hymns are especially suitable during the Epiphany season.

The English and Canadian books direct that the collect, epistle and gospel for the Epiphany be used until the following Sunday: the American book provides for the reading of the collect throughout the octave which includes, of course, the First Sunday after Epiphany.

The number of Sundays after Epiphany varies from one to six, depending upon whether Easter falls early or late. The simplest way to find the length of the Epiphany season and the dates of all moveable feasts until Trinity Sunday is to consult the tables: in the English and American books, *A Table of Moveable Feasts According to the Several Days that Easter Can Possibly Fall Upon;* in the Canadian book, *A Table of Moveable Feasts for One Hundred Years*. The calendar at the end of this chapter may also prove to be helpful.

§5 "Little Lent"

Epiphany-tide is followed by a short period unofficially known as "Little Lent," and designated in the American book as The Pre-

Lenten Season. In it occur three Sundays called, respectively, Septuagesima, Sexagesima and Quinquagesima, the dates of which may be found by consulting the tables of moveable feasts.

Septuagesima is the ninth Sunday before Easter. Traditional hymns for this day dwell upon the theme of God as Creator, the reference being in harmony with the lessons from the Old Testament which, in the English and Canadian churches, are from the first and second chapters of Genesis. Less stress may be laid upon this theme in the American church which uses other lessons for the day, although the earlier chapters of Genesis are appointed to be read on the Monday after Septuagesima.

It should be noted that no *Alleluias* are sung from Septuagesima until Easter. There is no direction in the Prayer Books relating to this custom, but it is an old tradition that is observed with good reason. The pre-Lenten season and Lent itself are penitential periods, and the singing of joyful *Alleluias* would scarcely be consistent with the meditative nature of the services. At one time, some churches used to make a ceremony of "burying the Alleluia" during the week before Septuagesima, and "resurrecting" it early on Easter morning. Many Anglican hymnals still contain a hymn which was sung during the "burying of the Alleluia," and which reads in part:

Alleluia cannot always
  Be our song while here below;
Alleluia our transgressions
  Make us for a while forego;
For the solemn time is coming
  When our tears for sin must flow.

The dominant theme of Sexagesima Sunday is that of the gospel: the Sower and the Seed.

On Quinquagesima the subject of charity is brought to mind by the collect and epistle. There is no lack of hymns and anthems based upon the theme of brotherly love.

§6 Lent

The Wednesday following Quinquagesima Sunday is Ash Wednesday, the first day of Lent. Some time before, the choirmaster should have made any necessary preparation for the Commination Service (or Penitential Office, as it is known in the American church) which is appointed for use on Ash Wednesday.

Lent is a season of fasting and abstinence, patterned after our Lord's forty days of fasting in the wilderness. Actually there are forty-six days from Ash Wednesday to Easter, since the six Sundays which intervene are regarded (like all Sundays) as feast days, and therefore are not to be included among the forty fast days.

Every Anglican hymnal contains a section devoted to Lenten hymns and a list of other hymns suitable for the season. These, with the lessons, collects, epistles and gospels should furnish the choirmaster with a reliable guide as to the type of anthem to choose. It might be remarked that Lenten music, although solemn, need not be doleful.

The penitential character of the season is generally maintained on Sundays in Lent, even though they are not fast days. If daily services are held, a slightly brighter note may be introduced on Sundays (avoiding music of a triumphal nature, of course); but where services are held only on Sundays, the solemnity of the season should be strictly observed, since there are no other opportunities for Lenten devotions.

In the English and Canadian churches, the collect for Ash Wednesday is used daily in addition to the collect for the day from the First Sunday in Lent (sometimes called Quadragesima) until Easter Even; but in the American church, only until Palm Sunday.

The Wednesday, Friday and Saturday after the First Sunday in Lent are Ember Days, when again the clergy, candidates for Holy Orders, and church workers in general are remembered. In the Canadian church, the consecutive readings in the *Table of Lessons* may be continued uninterrupted, or those listed under *Proper Lessons for Special Days* may be used; in the American book, Ember Days are provided for in the *Psalms and Lessons for the Christian Year*. In both the Canadian and American churches the same collect, epistle and gospel as used for Ember Days in Advent are read. In the English church the collect, epistle and gospel for the previous Sunday serve for the entire week.

In olden times, the Fourth Sunday in Lent was known as Mothering Sunday, from the theme of the epistle for the day, and the traditional name is still retained in some localities. It was the custom for members of the family who had left home to return and spend this day with their parents, much as Mothers' Day is now observed in Canada and the United States. Hymns referring to the Church or Jerusalem as the mother or home of the faithful are appropriate.

The Fifth Sunday in Lent, called Passion Sunday, brings the shadow of the Cross. Hymns and anthems should be meditations on the passion of Christ, and of His approaching sacrifice.

The Sixth Sunday in Lent, known as Palm Sunday, commemorates Christ's triumphal entry into Jerusalem. All Anglican hymnals designate suitable hymns.

Following Palm Sunday is Holy Week, a very busy time for organists and choirs of most parishes.

For Monday, Tuesday, Wednesday and Thursday of Holy Week, epistles and gospels only are provided in the English and Canadian books, the collects being those of Palm Sunday and Ash Wednesday. The American book provides a collect for each day which is followed by the collect for Palm Sunday.

Good Friday has three collects, and Easter Even (Saturday) one. These are followed by the collect for Ash Wednesday in the English and Canadian churches, but by no additional collects in the American church.

§7 Easter-tide

Easter Day surely requires little comment. Music that echoes the triumph of the Resurrection fills all Christian churches, and joyful *Alleluias* are heard once more.

The American book contains an alternative collect, epistle and gospel to be used when there is more than one Communion service on Easter Day.

The Monday and Tuesday after Easter are Holy Days for which epistles and gospels are provided. The American book provides collects for these days also. The collect for Easter Day serves for the entire week in the English and Canadian churches, and is used as an additional collect on Monday and Tuesday in the American church.

The Easter season lasts for five weeks, and seasonal music may be sung throughout. In a sense, every Sunday is a commemoration of Easter, and it is always appropriate to sing hymns that bring to mind the Resurrection. However, many prefer to reserve hymns linking the words "resurrection" and "today" (such as "Christ the Lord is risen today") for use on Easter Day only. This restriction, if observed, does not result in any scarcity of suitable music for Sundays after Easter.

Opportunities may be found for using hymns that mention post-Resurrection incidents which form the subjects of gospels and lessons. For instance, the lectionaries of all three Prayer Books appoint the latter part of the twentieth chapter of St. John, which tells of the doubt and reassurance of Thomas, as the second lesson at Evening Prayer on the First Sunday after Easter. No more appropriate hymn could be found than "O sons and daughters, let us sing!" which re-tells the whole story and thus impresses it more deeply on the minds of the people. The hymn for St. Thomas' Day will serve the same purpose.

The story of the walk to Emmaus, which is read in the American church on Easter Sunday evening, and in the Canadian church on the morning of the First Sunday after Easter, is another for which suitable hymns may be found. Such opportunities for harmonizing various parts of the service abound for the choirmaster who will take care in choosing his hymns.

On the Second Sunday after Easter it is customary to use some hymns, and perhaps an anthem, whose subject is Christ the Good Shepherd, that being the theme of the gospel.

The Fifth Sunday after Easter is called Rogation Sunday, and the three days following are Rogation Days. At this time the church asks God's blessing on the seeding, and intercessions are made for the general prosperity and welfare of the nation. In the Canadian and American books are found a collect, epistle and gospel for the Rogation Days: in the English church, the collect, epistle and gospel for the Fifth Sunday after Easter are used.

§8 Ascension-tide

The Thursday immediately following the Rogation Days is observed as Ascension Day, a major festival of the church for which ample material is provided in the hymnals under the seasonal heading.

On the Sunday after Ascension Day, the same theme is continued—in fact, many churches which cannot muster congregations for week-day services have their principal Ascension-tide celebrations on this Sunday following the festival. In the American church, the collect for Ascension Day (which is used throughout the octave) follows the collect for the Sunday.

§9 Whitsun-tide

Whit Sunday, or the Feast of Pentecost, occurs ten days after Ascension Day, and commemorates the descent of the Holy Spirit. Epistles and gospels are appointed for the Monday and Tuesday in Whitsun week; and the American book provides new collects, also, which are followed by the collect for Whit Sunday. It will be noted that the American book contains also an alternative collect, epistle and gospel to be used at a second celebration of the Holy Communion on Whit Sunday.

The Wednesday, Friday and Saturday after Whit Sunday are Ember Days. The Canadian and American books provide lessons and the same collect, epistle and gospel that are used for Ember Days in Advent are again read. The American book directs that the collect for Whit Sunday be used throughout the week (in addition to any others appointed) and the same practice is generally followed in the Canadian church.

§10 The Trinity Season

Following Whitsun week is Trinity Sunday, emphasizing the three-fold nature of God. Hymns and anthems which dwell upon any one Person of the Trinity are not appropriate.

The rest of the Sundays in the church year are known as Sundays after Trinity. Music may be of a general nature, although a continued study of the lessons, collects, epistles and gospels will result in a better selection of appropriate hymns and anthems.

The number of Sundays after Trinity depends upon the date of Easter. If Easter is early, there may be as many as twenty-seven Sundays after Trinity; if late, there may be as few as twenty-two. All Prayer Books provide lessons for twenty-seven Sundays after Trinity, but collects, epistles and gospels for only twenty-five. Since a long Trinity season can occur only when there has been a short Epiphany season, the collects, epistles and gospels which were omitted during Epiphany are used on Sundays after Trinity for which none are provided.

The rubrics after the collect, epistle and gospel for the Twenty-Fifth Sunday after Trinity in the English book, after those of the Sunday next before Advent in the Canadian book, and after those of the Twenty-Fourth Sunday after Trinity in the American book explain clearly the use of Epiphany-tide collects, epistles and gospels during a long Trinity season.

During the Trinity season occur three more Ember Days: the Wednesday, Friday and Saturday after September 14. The English church uses the collect, epistle and gospel of the preceding Sunday; the Canadian and American churches, the collect, epistle and gospel appointed for all Ember Days.

§11 Saints' Days and Other Holy Days

In addition to the Sundays and Holy Days already mentioned, there are a number of other festivals for which collects, epistles and gospels are provided. (The reader is referred to the *Tables and Rules for the Moveable and Immoveable Feasts, Together with the Days of Fasting and Abstinence Through the Whole Year* which appear in all Prayer Books.)

Some Holy Days have vigils or eves which are observed as fast days: some have not. In the *Tables and Rules for Feasts, etc.* mentioned above, the English and Canadian books list the vigils among the days of fasting and abstinence: the American book omits the vigils in these tables but recognizes them in the *Psalms and Lessons for Fixed Holy Days* by providing lessons for them.

The English book, in the table of *Lessons Proper for Holy Days*, appoints lessons for the festivals only, not the vigils: the Canadian and American books list lessons for the evenings preceding Holy Days whether these eves are fasts or not.

In general, when a Holy Day falls upon a Monday its vigil or eve is observed on the previous Saturday, since Sunday cannot be a fast day. In such a case, however, the collect for the Holy Day will probably be used on Sunday evening; and in churches where services are not held daily, the lessons at Evening Prayer on Sunday may be those of the Holy Day or its vigil. Customs vary, and the choirmaster should consult his rector as to the policy to be followed in the observance of Holy Days. In any case, it is quite appropriate to have a hymn for the Holy Day on the Sunday nearest its observance.

Very often a Holy Day will occur upon a Sunday, or during a season too important to be neglected, in which case the Holy Day may be transferred to a convenient date. However, if a Holy Day falls upon one of certain other Sundays, it is observed in preference to the Sunday. The Canadian and American books contain tables directing which festival is to be given precedence when two fall upon the same day.

Most hymnals have hymns for each of the Holy Days in the following list, and others may be selected from hymns for apostles, evangelists, martyrs, etc.

Except where noted, the collects, epistles and gospels for these

Holy Days are found in the Prayer Books after those of the Sundays after Trinity. Those with vigils are so indicated.

St. Andrew, Apostle and Martyr, (Vigil) November 30, falling upon the First Sunday in Advent, is transferred to the Monday following, although the collect may be read on the Sunday. When it is celebrated on any day during the week after Advent Sunday, the collect for the Sunday will follow that of the saint's day.

St. Andrew's Day often occurs before Advent, in which case it is not necessary to read any collect but that of the Holy Day.

St. Thomas, Apostle and Martyr, (Vigil) December 21, always occurs during Advent, and its collect is followed by that of the First Sunday in Advent, and perhaps by that of the preceding Sunday as well. If the saint's day falls upon the Fourth Sunday in Advent, it is transferred to Monday.

St. Thomas' Day may also occur on an Ember Day, in which case it is given precedence.

St. Stephen, Deacon and Martyr, December 26, *St. John, Apostle and Evangelist,* December 27, and *The Holy Innocents,* December 28, were mentioned in the section devoted to Christmastide, since their collects, epistles and gospels follow those of Christmas Day.

Conversion of St. Paul, January 25, takes precedence if it occurs on a Sunday in the Epiphany season; but is transferred to Monday if it falls upon Septuagesima or Sexagesima Sundays. Missionary hymns are appropriate for this festival.

Purification of the Blessed Virgin Mary, (Vigil) February 2, sometimes called the *Presentation of Christ in the Temple,* is given precedence when it occurs on a Sunday in the Epiphany season, but is postponed a day when it falls upon Septuagesima, Sexagesima or Quinquagesima Sundays.

St. Matthias, Apostle and Martyr, (Vigil) February 24, is transferred to a day later when it falls upon Sexagesima or Quinquagesima Sundays, Ash Wednesday, or a Sunday in Lent. When observed in Lent, its collect is followed by that of Ash Wednesday.

Annunciation of the Blessed Virgin Mary, (Vigil) March 25, is transferred more often than any other Holy Day. When it occurs on the Third, Fourth or Fifth Sundays in Lent it is transferred to the next day; when it falls upon any day from Palm Sunday to the First Sunday after Easter, it is transferred to the second Monday after Easter. When observed in Lent its collect is, of course, followed by that of Ash Wednesday.

St. Mark, Evangelist and Martyr, April 25, falling upon Easter Day or any of the seven days following Easter, is transferred to the second Monday after Easter unless that happens to be St. Philip and St. James' Day, in which case St. Mark's Day is transferred to the second Tuesday after Easter.

St. Mark's Day takes precedence over the Second, Third and Fourth Sundays after Easter and, in the Canadian church, over the Fifth Sunday after Easter also. The American book gives precedence to the Fifth Sunday after Easter, and directs that any other festival falling on that Sunday be transferred to the first convenient open day, which would be the following Friday.

St. Philip and St. James, Apostles and Martyrs, May 1, occurring on the Saturday or Sunday after Easter is transferred to the following Tuesday (St. Mark's Day will have been transferred to Monday); when on Ascension Day, it is transferred to the following day.

The saint's day takes precedence over the Second, Third and Fourth Sundays after Easter and, in the Canadian church, over the Fifth Sunday after Easter. In the American church, when the festival falls upon the Fifth Sunday after Easter, it is transferred to the following Friday.

The transference of St. Mark's Day or St. Philip and St. James' Day from the Fifth Sunday after Easter to the following Friday is suggested in the belief that most clergymen would prefer to observe the Rogation Days on Monday, Tuesday and Wednesday. However, it would be quite logical to transfer the red letter day to Monday, since St. Philip and St. James' Day is given precedence when it falls on a Rogation Day. The choirmaster must consult his own rector when any doubt arises.

St. Barnabas, Apostle and Martyr, June 11, occurring on any day from Whit Sunday to Trinity Sunday is transferred to the Monday after Trinity Sunday. It takes precedence over Sundays after Trinity.

The following Holy Days always occur in the Trinity season and are given precedence when they fall upon Sundays:

Nativity of St. John the Baptist, (Vigil) June 24
St. Peter, Apostle and Martyr, (Vigil) June 29
St. James, Apostle and Martyr, (Vigil) July 25
Transfiguration of our Lord, August 6
St. Bartholomew, Apostle and Martyr, (Vigil) August 24
St. Matthew, Apostle, Evangelist and Martyr, (Vigil) September 21
St. Michael and All Angels, September 29
St. Luke, Evangelist, October 18
St. Simon and St. Jude, Apostles and Martyrs, (Vigil) October 28
All Saints, (Vigil) November 1

§12 Black Letter Days

The church calendar lists also a number of lesser days of commemoration which are known as black letter days, to distinguish them from the major festivals whose dates are often printed in red.

These lesser days are not generally observed unless they are patronal festivals (that is, days of saints after whom churches are named, such as St. Chad, St. Margaret, St. Alban, St. George, etc.). If they are observed, the choirmaster will have to ask his rector what lessons, collects, epistles and gospels are to be used.

The American Prayer Book lists five sets of lessons for patronal festivals (for a bishop, a confessor, a martyr, a virgin and a matron) which will suggest appropriate hymns for the occasions; and a collect, epistle and gospel for a Saint's Day which is suitable for any saint's day not otherwise provided for.

§13 Special Services

Lessons, collects, epistles and gospels are provided for other occasional services: in all Prayer Books for the Ordering of Deacons and Priests, and the Consecration of Bishops; in the Canadian and American books, for the Induction of Ministers, Consecration of a Church, and for communions at weddings and funerals.

The Canadian book provides lessons, collect, epistle and gospel for a Special Service for Missions; and the American book suggests lessons to be used before confirmations, ordinations and consecrations, at the institution of ministers, at church conventions, mission services, and gatherings for Christian education and social service.

§14 National Observances

The English and Canadian books provide for a service on the anniversary of the accession of the reigning sovereign; the Canadian and American books for Thanksgiving Day (or Harvest Festival) and the national holidays—Dominion Day (July 1) in Canada, and Independence Day (July 4) in the United States. The American book lists lessons for other national and state festivals and fasts.

While the church seasons and Holy Days may seem a little confusing to one who has hitherto been unacquainted with them, persistence will soon result in familiarity. The calendar at the end of this chapter, to which reference has already been made, owes its size and bulk to the fact that no effort was spared to include in it the answers to any questions or problems that might arise concerning the church's seasonal observances.

Church Calendar

TABLE I
Sundays and Holy Days which do not occur on the same date every year

TABLE II
Sundays and Holy Days which are sometimes transferred from their fixed dates

TABLE III
Holy Days with fixed dates which are never transferred

TABLE I: *SUNDAYS AND HOLY DAYS WHICH DO*

When Easter falls upon	*Mar.22*	*Mar.23*	*Mar.24*	*Mar.25*	*Mar.26*	*Mar.27*	*Mar.28*
1st Sunday in Advent	Nov.30†	Dec. 1	Dec. 2	Dec. 3	Nov.27	Nov.28	Nov.29
2nd Sunday in Advent	Dec. 7	8	9	10	Dec. 4	Dec. 5	Dec. 6
3rd Sunday in Advent	14	15	16	17	11	12	13
Ember Days in Advent	17	18	19	20	14	15	16
	19	20	21*	22	16	17	18
	20	21*	22	23	17	18	19
4th Sunday in Advent	21†	22	23	24	18	19	20
1st Sunday after Christmas	28*a*	29	30	31	Jan. 1*	26*a*	27*a*
2nd Sunday after Christmas	Jan. 4	Jan. 5	—	—	—	Jan. 2	Jan. 3
1st Sunday after Epiphany	11	12	Jan. 13	Jan. 7	Jan. 8	9	10
2nd Sunday after Epiphany	—	—	—	14	15	16	17
3rd Sunday after Epiphany	—	—	—	—	—	—	—
4th Sunday after Epiphany	—	—	—	—	—	—	—
5th Sunday after Epiphany	—	—	—	—	—	—	—
6th Sunday after Epiphany	—	—	—	—	—	—	—
Septuagesima Sunday	Jan. 18	Jan. 19	Jan. 20	Jan. 21	Jan. 22	Jan. 23	Jan. 24
Sexagesima Sunday	25†	26	27	28	29	30	31
Quinquagesima Sunday	Feb. 1	Feb. 2†	Feb. 3	Feb. 4	Feb. 5	Feb. 6	Feb. 7
Ash Wednesday	4	5	6	7	8	9	10
1st Sunday in Lent	8	9	10	11	12	13	14
Ember Days in Lent	11	12	13	14	15	16	17
	13	14	15	16	17	18	19
	14	15	16	17	18	19	20
2nd Sunday in Lent	15	16	17	18	19	20	21
3rd Sunday in Lent	22	23	24†	25	26	27	28
4th Sunday in Lent	Mar. 1	Mar. 2	Mar. 3	Mar. 4	Mar. 5	Mar. 6	Mar. 7
5th Sunday in Lent	8	9	10	11	12	13	14
6th Sunday in Lent	15	16	17	18	19	20	21
Good Friday	20	21	22	23	24	25†	26
Easter Day	22	23	24	25†	26	27	28
1st Sunday after Easter	29	30	31	Apr. 1	Apr. 2	Apr. 3	Apr. 4
2nd Sunday after Easter	Apr. 5	Apr. 6	Apr. 7	8	9	10	11
3rd Sunday after Easter	12	13	14	15	16	17	18
4th Sunday after Easter	19	20	21	22	23	24	25*
5th Sunday after Easter	26	27	28	29	30	May 1*	May 2
Rogation Days	27	28	29	30	May 1*	2	3
	28	29	30	May 1*	2	3	4
	29	30	May 1*	2	3	4	5
Ascension Day	30	May 1†	2	3	4	5	6
Sunday after Ascension Day	May 3	4	5	6	7	8	9
Whit Sunday	10	11	12	13	14	15	16
Ember Days in Whitsuntide	13	14	15	16	17	18	19
	15	16	17	18	19	20	21
	16	17	18	19	20	21	22
Trinity Sunday	17	18	19	20	21	22	23
Number of Sundays after Trinity	27	27	27	27	27	26	26
Sundays after Trinity on which precedence is given to other Holy Days (See Table III)	Oct. 18* Nov. 1*	Jun. 29* Aug.24* Sep. 21*	Sep. 29*	Jun. 24* Oct. 28*	Jun. 11* Aug. 6*		Jul. 25*
Autumnal Ember Days	Sep. 16	Sep. 17	Sep. 18	Sep. 19	Sep. 20	Sep. 21*	Sep. 15
	18	19	20	21*	22	23	17
	19	20	21*	22	23	24	18
21st Sunday after Trinity	Oct. 11	Oct. 12	Oct. 13	Oct. 14	Oct. 15	Oct. 16	Oct. 17
22nd Sunday after Trinity	18*	19	20	21	22	23	24
23rd Sunday after Trinity	25	26	27	28*	29	30	31
24th Sunday after Trinity	Nov. 1*	Nov. 2	Nov. 3	Nov. 4	Nov. 5	Nov. 6	Nov. 7
25th Sunday after Trinity	8*c*	9*c*	10*c*	11*c*	12*c*	13*b*	14*b*
26th Sunday after Trinity	15*b*	16*b*	17*b*	18*b*	19*b*	—	—
Sunday next before Advent	22	23	24	25	26	Nov.20	Nov.21

TO USE THIS CALENDAR: Determine the date of Easter. In the column headed by that date is found the church calendar for the entire year, from the Advent Sunday preceding Easter's date to the Sunday before the next Advent season.

NOT OCCUR ON THE SAME DATE EVERY YEAR

Mar.29	*Mar.30*	*Mar.31*	*Apr. 1*	*Apr. 2*	*Apr. 3*	*Apr. 4*	*Apr. 5*	*Apr. 6*	*Apr. 7*	*Apr. 8*
Nov.30†	Dec. 1	Dec. 2	Dec. 3	Nov.27	Nov.28	Nov.29	Nov.30†	Dec. 1	Dec. 2	Dec. 3
Dec. 7	8	9	10	Dec. 4	Dec. 5	Dec. 6	Dec. 7	8	9	10
14	15	16	17	11	12	13	14	15	16	17
17	18	19	20	14	15	16	17	18	19	20
19	20	21*	22	16	17	18	19	20	21*	22
20	21*	22	23	17	18	19	20	21*	22	23
21†	22	23	24	18	19	20	21†	22	23	24
28*a*	29	30	31	Jan. 1*	26*a*	27*a*	28*a*	29	30	31
Jan. 4	Jan. 5	—	—	—	Jan. 2	Jan. 3	Jan. 4	Jan. 5	—	—
11	12	Jan. 13	Jan. 7	Jan. 8	9	10	11	12	Jan. 13	Jan. 7
18	19	20	14	15	16	17	18	19	20	14
—	—	—	21	22	23	24	25*	26	27	21
—	—	—	—	—	—	—	—	—	—	28
—	—	—	—	—	—	—	—	—	—	—
—	—	—	—	—	—	—	—	—	—	—
Jan. 25†	Jan. 26	Jan. 27	Jan. 28	Jan. 29	Jan. 30	Jan. 31	Feb. 1	Feb. 2†	Feb. 3	Feb. 4
Feb. 1	Feb. 2†	Feb. 3	Feb. 4	Feb. 5	Feb. 6	Feb. 7	8	9	10	11
8	9	10	11	12	13	14	15	16	17	18
11	12	13	14	15	16	17	18	19	20	21
15	16	17	18	19	20	21	22	23	24†	25
18	19	20	21	22	23	24*	25	26	27	28
20	21	22	23	24*	25	26	27	28	Mar. 1	Mar. 2
21	22	23	24*	25	26	27	28	Mar. 1	2	3
22	23	24†	25	26	27	28	Mar. 1	2	3	4
Mar. 1	Mar. 2	Mar. 3	Mar. 4	Mar. 5	Mar. 6	Mar. 7	8	9	10	11
8	9	10	11	12	13	14	15	16	17	18
15	16	17	18	19	20	21	22	23	24	25†
22	23	24	25†	26	27	28	29	30	31	Apr. 1
27	28	29	30	31	Apr. 1	Apr. 2	Apr. 3	Apr. 4	Apr. 5	6
29	30	31	Apr. 1	Apr. 2	3	4	5	6	7	8
Apr. 5	Apr. 6	Apr. 7	8	9	10	11	12	13	14	15
12	13	14	15	16	17	18	19	20	21	22
19	20	21	22	23	24	25*	26	27	28	29
26	27	28	29	30	May 1*	May 2	May 3	May 4	May 5	May 6
May 3	May 4	May 5	May 6	May 7	8	9	10	11	12	13
4	5	6	7	8	9	10	11	12	13	14
5	6	7	8	9	10	11	12	13	14	15
6	7	8	9	10	11	12	13	14	15	16
7	8	9	10	11	12	13	14	15	16	17
10	11	12	13	14	15	16	17	18	19	20
17	18	19	20	21	22	23	24	25	26	27
20	21	22	23	24	25	26	27	28	29	30
22	23	24	25	26	27	28	29	30	31	Jun. 1
23	24	25	26	27	28	29	30	31	Jun. 1	2
24	25	26	27	28	29	30	31	Jun. 1	2	3
26	26	26	26	26	25	25	25	25	25	25
Oct. 18*	Jun. 29*	Sep. 29*	Jun. 24*	Jun. 11*		Jul. 25*	Oct. 18*	Jun. 29*	Sep. 29*	Jun. 24*
Nov. 1*	Aug.24*		Oct. 28*	Aug. 6*			Nov. 1*	Aug.24*		Oct. 28*
	Sep. 21*							Sep. 21*		
Sep. 16	Sep. 17	Sep. 18	Sep. 19	Sep. 20	Sep. 21*	Sep. 15	Sep. 16	Sep. 17	Sep. 18	Sep. 19
18	19	20	21*	22	23	17	18	19	20	21*
19	20	21*	22	23	24	18	19	20	21*	22
Oct. 18*	Oct. 19	Oct. 20	Oct. 21	Oct. 22	Oct. 23	Oct. 24	Oct. 25	Oct. 26	Oct. 27	Oct. 28*
25	26	27	28*	29	30	31	Nov. 1*	Nov. 2	Nov. 3	Nov. 4
Nov. 1*	Nov. 2	Nov. 3	Nov. 4	Nov. 5	Nov. 6	Nov. 7	8	9	10	11
8	9	10	11	12	13	14	15	16	17	18
15*b*	16*b*	17*b*	18*b*	19*b*	—	—	—	—	—	—
—	—	—	—	—	—	—	—	—	—	—
Nov.22	Nov.23	Nov.24	Nov.25	Nov.26	Nov.20	Nov.21	Nov.22	Nov.23	Nov.24	Nov.25

FOR A LEAP YEAR: Read the column to the *right* of that headed by the date of Easter until March 1 (read February 29 for March 1); then, on March 1, revert to the column headed by the date on which Easter falls.

TABLE I: *SUNDAYS AND HOLY DAYS WHICH DO NOT*

	Apr. 9	*Apr. 10*	*Apr. 11*	*Apr. 12*	*Apr. 13*	*Apr. 14*	*Apr. 15*
1st Sunday in Advent	Nov. 27	Nov. 28	Nov. 29	Nov. 30†	Dec. 1	Dec. 2	Dec. 3
2nd Sunday in Advent	Dec. 4	Dec. 5	Dec. 6	Dec. 7	8	9	10
3rd Sunday in Advent	11	12	13	14	15	16	17
	14	15	16	17	18	19	20
Ember Days in Advent	16	17	18	19	20	21*	22
	17	18	19	20	21*	22	23
4th Sunday in Advent	18	19	20	21†	22	23	24
1st Sunday after Christmas	Jan. 1*	*26a*	*27a*	*28a*	29	30	31
2nd Sunday after Christmas	—	Jan. 2	Jan. 3	Jan. 4	Jan. 5	—	—
1st Sunday after Epiphany	Jan. 8	9	10	11	12	Jan. 13	Jan. 7
2nd Sunday after Epiphany	15	16	17	18	19	20	14
3rd Sunday after Epiphany	22	23	24	25*	26	27	21
4th Sunday after Epiphany	29	30	31	Feb. 1	Feb. 2*	Feb. 3	28
5th Sunday after Epiphany	—	—	—	—	—	—	Feb. 4
6th Sunday after Epiphany	—	—	—	—	—	—	—
Septuagesima Sunday	Feb. 5	Feb. 6	Feb. 7	Feb. 8	Feb. 9	Feb. 10	Feb. 11
Sexagesima Sunday	12	13	14	15	16	17	18
Quinquagesima Sunday	19	20	21	22	23	24†	25
Ash Wednesday	22	23	24†	25	26	27	28
1st Sunday in Lent	26	27	28	Mar. 1	Mar. 2	Mar. 3	Mar. 4
	Mar. 1	Mar. 2	Mar. 3	4	5	6	7
Ember Days in Lent	3	4	5	6	7	8	9
	4	5	6	7	8	9	10
2nd Sunday in Lent	5	6	7	8	9	10	11
3rd Sunday in Lent	12	13	14	15	16	17	18
4th Sunday in Lent	19	20	21	22	23	24	25†
5th Sunday in Lent	26	27	28	29	30	31	Apr. 1
6th Sunday in Lent	Apr. 2	Apr. 3	Apr. 4	Apr. 5	Apr. 6	Apr. 7	8
Good Friday	7	8	9	10	11	12	13
Easter Day	9	10	11	12	13	14	15
1st Sunday after Easter	16	17	18	19	20	21	22
2nd Sunday after Easter	23	24	25*	26	27	28	29
3rd Sunday after Easter	30	May 1*	May 2	May 3	May 4	May 5	May 6
4th Sunday after Easter	May 7	May 8	9	10	11	12	13
5th Sunday after Easter	14	15	16	17	18	19	20
	15	16	17	18	19	20	21
Rogation Days	16	17	18	19	20	21	22
	17	18	19	20	21	22	23
Ascension Day	18	19	20	21	22	23	24
Sunday after Ascension Day	21	22	23	24	25	26	27
Whit Sunday	28	29	30	31	Jun. 1	Jun. 2	Jun. 3
	31	Jun. 1	Jun. 2	Jun. 3	4	5	6
Ember Days in Whitsuntide	Jun. 2	3	4	5	6	7	8
	3	4	5	6	7	8	9
Trinity Sunday	4	5	6	7	8	9	10
Number of Sundays after Trinity	25	24	24	24	24	24	24
Sundays after Trinity on which precedence is given to other Holy Days (See Table III)	Jun. 11*		Jul. 25*	Oct. 18*	Jun. 29*	Sep. 29*	Jun. 24*
	Aug. 6*			Nov. 1*	Aug. 24*		
					Sep. 21*		Oct. 28*
	Sep. 20	Sep. 21*	Sep. 15	Sep. 16	Sep. 17	Sep. 18	Sep. 19
Autumnal Ember Days	22	23	17	18	19	20	21*
	23	24	18	19	20	21*	22
21st Sunday after Trinity	Oct. 29	Oct. 30	Oct. 31	Nov. 1*	Nov. 2	Nov. 3	Nov. 4
22nd Sunday after Trinity	Nov. 5	Nov. 6	Nov. 7	8	9	10	11
23rd Sunday after Trinity	12	13	14	15	16	17	18
24th Sunday after Trinity	19	—	—	—	—	—	—
25th Sunday after Trinity	—	—	—	—	—	—	—
26th Sunday after Trinity	—	—	—	—	—	—	—
Sunday next before Advent	Nov. 26	Nov. 20	Nov. 21	Nov. 22	Nov. 23	Nov. 24	Nov. 25

* Sundays and Holy Days marked thus in this table give place to Saints' Days and other Holy Days with fixed dates (See Tables II and III).

† Sundays and Holy Days marked thus in this table take precedence over other Holy Days falling upon the same dates.

a The American Prayer Book directs that the Feasts of St. Stephen, St. John the Evangelist and the Holy Innocents be observed and given precedence when they occur on the First

OCCUR ON THE SAME DATE EVERY YEAR (continued)

Apr. 16	*Apr. 17*	*Apr. 18*	*Apr. 19*	*Apr. 20*	*Apr. 21*	*Apr. 22*	*Apr. 23*	*Apr. 24*	*Apr. 25*	*A Leap Year*
Nov.27	Nov.28	Nov.29	Nov.30†	Dec. 1	Dec. 2	Dec. 3	Nov.27	Nov.28	Nov.29	Nov.30†
Dec. 4	Dec. 5	Dec. 6	Dec. 7	8	9	10	Dec. 4	Dec. 5	Dec. 6	Dec. 7
11	12	13	14	15	16	17	11	12	13	14
14	15	16	17	18	19	20	14	15	16	17 }
16	17	18	19	20	21*	22	16	17	18	19 }
17	18	19	20	21*	22	23	17	18	19	20 }
18	19	20	21†	22	23	24	18	19	20	21†
Jan. 1*	26*a*	27*a*	28*a*	29	30	31	Jan. 1*	26*a*	27*a*	28*a*
—	Jan. 2	Jan. 3	Jan. 4	Jan. 5	—	—	—	Jan. 2	Jan. 3	Jan. 4
Jan. 8	9	10	11	12	Jan. 13	Jan. 7	Jan. 8	Jan. 9	Jan. 10	Jan. 11
15	16	17	18	19	20	14	15	16	17	18
22	23	24	25*	26	27	21	22	23	24	25*
29	30	31	Feb. 1	Feb. 2*	Feb. 3	28	29	30	31	Feb. 1
Feb. 5	Feb. 6	Feb. 7	8	9	10	Feb. 4	Feb. 5	Feb. 6	Feb. 7	8
—	—	—	—	—	—	11	12	13	14	15
Feb. 12	Feb. 13	Feb. 14	Feb. 15	Feb. 16	Feb. 17	18	19	20	21	22
19	20	21	22	23	24†	25	26	27	28	29
26	27	28	Mar. 1	Mar. 2	Mar. 3	Mar. 4	Mar. 5	Mar. 6	Mar. 7	—
Mar. 1	Mar. 2	Mar. 3	Mar. 4	5	6	7	8	9	10	—
5	6	7	8	9	10	11	12	13	14	—
8	9	10	11	12	13	14	15	16	17	— }
10	11	12	13	14	15	16	17	18	19	— }
11	12	13	14	15	16	17	18	19	20	— }
12	13	14	15	16	17	18	19	20	21	—
19	20	21	22	23	24	25†	26	27	28	—
26	27	28	29	30	31	Apr. 1	Apr. 2	Apr. 3	Apr. 4	—
Apr. 2	Apr. 3	Apr. 4	Apr. 5	Apr. 6	Apr. 7	8	9	10	11	—
9	10	11	12	13	14	15	16	17	18	—
14	15	16	17	18	19	20	21	22	23	—
16	17	18	19	20	21	22	23	24	25†	—
23	24	25†	26	27	28	29	30	May 1†	May 2	—
30	May 1*	May 2	May 3	May 4	May 5	May 6	May 7	8	9	—
May 7	8	9	10	11	12	13	14	15	16	—
14	15	16	17	18	19	20	21	22	23	—
21	22	23	24	25	26	27	28	29	30	—
22	23	24	25	26	27	28	29	30	31	— }
23	24	25	26	27	28	29	30	31	Jun. 1	— }
24	25	26	27	28	29	30	31	Jun. 1	2	— }
25	26	27	28	29	30	31	Jun. 1	2	3	—
28	29	30	31	Jun. 1	Jun. 2	Jun. 3	4	5	6	—
Jun. 4	Jun. 5	Jun. 6	Jun. 7	8	9	10	11†	12	13	—
7	8	9	10	11†	12	13	14	15	16	— }
9	10	11†	12	13	14	15	16	17	18	— }
10	11†	12	13	14	15	16	17	18	19	— }
11†	12	13	14	15	16	17	18	19	20	—
24	23	23	23	23	23	23	23	22	22	—
Aug. 6*		Jul. 25*	Oct. 18*	Jun. 29*	Sep. 29*	Jun. 24*	Aug. 6*		Jul. 25*	—
			Nov. 1*	Aug. 24*		Oct. 28*				
				Sep. 21*						
Sep. 20	Sep. 21*	Sep. 15	Sep. 16	Sep. 17	Sep. 18	Sep. 19	Sep. 20	Sep. 21*	Sep. 15	— }
22	23	17	18	19	20	21*	22	23	17	— }
23	24	18	19	20	21*	22	23	24	18	— }
Nov. 5	Nov. 6	Nov. 7	Nov. 8	Nov. 9	Nov.10	Nov.11	Nov.12	Nov.13	Nov.14	—
12	13	14	15	16	17	18	19	—	—	—
19	—	—	—	—	—	—	—	—	—	—
—	—	—	—	—	—	—	—	—	—	—
—	—	—	—	—	—	—	—	—	—	—
—	—	—	—	—	—	—	—	—	—	—
Nov.26	Nov.20	Nov.21	Nov.22	Nov.23	Nov.24	Nov.25	Nov.26	Nov.20	Nov.21	—

Sunday after Christmas; but the Canadian book gives precedence to the First Sunday after Christmas, and directs that any of the three Holy Days falling upon the same date be omitted for that year.

b The Collect, Epistle and Gospel for the Sixth Sunday after Epiphany are used.

c The Collect, Epistle and Gospel for the Fifth Sunday after Epiphany are used.

TABLE II: *HOLY DAYS WHICH ARE SOMETIMES*

When Easter falls upon	*Mar.22*	*Mar.23*	*Mar.24*	*Mar.25*	*Mar.26*	*Mar.27*	*Mar.28*
St. Andrew	Dec. 1†	Nov.30	Nov.30	Nov.30	Nov.30	Nov.30	Nov.30
St. Thomas	Dec.22†	Dec.21*	Dec.21*	Dec.21	Dec.21	Dec.21	Dec.21
St. Stephen	26	26	26	26	26	26*a*	26
St. John the Evangelist	27	27	27	27	27	27	27*a*
The Holy Innocents	28*a*	28	28	28	28	28	28
Conversion of St. Paul	Jan. 26†	Jan. 25	Jan. 25	Jan. 25	Jan. 25	Jan. 25	Jan. 25
Purification of the Blessed Virgin Mary	Feb. 2	Feb. 3†	Feb. 2	Feb. 2	Feb. 2	Feb. 2	Feb. 2
St. Matthias	24	24	25†	24	24	24	24
Annunciation of the Blessed Virgin Mary	Mar.30†	Mar.31†	Apr. 1†	Apr. 2†	Apr. 3†	Apr. 4†	Apr. 5†
St. Mark	Apr.25	Apr.25	25	25	25	25	25*
St. Philip and St. James	May 1	May 2†	May 1*	May 1*	May 1*	May 1*	May 1
St. Barnabas	Jun.11	Jun.11	Jun.11	Jun.11	Jun.11*	Jun.11	Jun.11

	Apr. 9	*Apr.10*	*Apr.11*	*Apr.12*	*Apr.13*	*Apr.14*	*Apr.15*
St. Andrew	Nov.30	Nov.30	Nov.30	Dec. 1†	Nov.30	Nov.30	Nov.30
St. Thomas	Dec.21	Dec.21	Dec.21	Dec.22†	Dec.21*	Dec.21*	Dec.21
St. Stephen	26	26*a*	26	26	26	26	26
St. John the Evangelist	27	27	27*a*	27	27	27	27
The Holy Innocents	28	28	28	28*a*	28	28	28
Conversion of St. Paul	Jan.25	Jan.25	Jan.25	Jan.25*	Jan.25	Jan.25	Jan.25
Purification of the Blessed Virgin Mary	Feb. 2	Feb. 2	Feb. 2	Feb. 2	Feb. 2*	Feb. 2	Feb. 2
St. Matthias	24	24	25†	24	24	25†	24
Annunciation of the Blessed Virgin Mary	Mar.25	Mar.25	Mar.25	Mar.25	Mar.25	Mar.25	Mar.26†
St. Mark	Apr.25	Apr.25	Apr.25*	Apr.25	Apr.25	Apr.25	Apr.25
St. Philip and St. James	May 1	May 1*	May 1	May 1	May 1	May 1	May 1
St. Barnabas	Jun.11*	Jun.11	Jun.11	Jun.11	Jun.11	Jun.11	Jun.11

* Holy Days marked thus in this table are celebrated on their usual dates, and take precedence over Sundays or any other Holy Days that fall upon the same dates.

† Holy Days marked thus in this table are transferred from their usual dates to make room for Sundays or other Holy Days which fall upon those dates and are given precedence.

a The American Prayer Book directs that the Feasts of St. Stephen, St. John the Evangelist and the Holy Innocents be observed and given precedence when they occur on the First Sunday after Christmas: the Canadian book gives precedence to the First Sunday after Christmas, and directs that any of the three Holy Days falling upon the same date be omitted for that year.

TRANSFERRED FROM THEIR FIXED DATES

Mar.29	*Mar.30*	*Mar.31*	*Apr. 1*	*Apr. 2*	*Apr. 3*	*Apr. 4*	*Apr. 5*	*Apr. 6*	*Apr. 7*	*Apr. 8*
Dec. 1†	Nov.30	Nov.30	Nov.30	Nov.30	Nov.30	Nov.30	Dec. 1†	Nov.30	Nov.30	Nov.30
Dec. 22†	Dec. 21*	Dec. 21*	Dec. 21	Dec. 21	Dec. 21	Dec. 21	Dec. 22†	Dec. 21*	Dec. 21*	Dec. 21
26	26	26	26	26	26*a*	26	26	26	26	26
27	27	27	27	27	27	27*a*	27	27	27	27
28*a*	28	28	28	28	28	28	28*a*	28	28	28
Jan. 26†	Jan. 25	Jan. 25	Jan. 25	Jan. 25	Jan. 25	Jan. 25	Jan. 25*	Jan. 25	Jan. 25	Jan. 25
Feb. 2	Feb. 3†	Feb. 2	Feb. 2	Feb. 2	Feb. 2	Feb. 2	Feb. 2	Feb. 3†	Feb. 2	Feb. 2
24	24	25†	24*	24*	24	24*	24	24	25†	24
Apr. 6†	Apr. 7†	Apr. 8†	Apr. 9†	Mar.25	Mar.25	Mar.25	Mar.25	Mar.25	Mar.25	Mar.26†
25	25	25	25	Apr. 25	Apr. 25	Apr. 25*	Apr. 25	Apr. 25	Apr. 25	Apr. 25
May 1	May 1	May 1	May 1	May 1	May 1*	May 1	May 1	May 1	May 1	May 1
Jun. 11	Jun. 11	Jun. 11	Jun. 11	Jun. 11*	Jun. 11	Jun. 11	Jun. 11	Jun. 11	Jun. 11	Jun. 11

Apr.16	*Apr.17*	*Apr.18*	*Apr.19*	*Apr.20*	*Apr.21*	*Apr.22*	*Apr.23*	*Apr.24*	*Apr.25*	*A Leap Year (e)*
Nov.30	Nov.30	Nov.30	Dec. 1†	Nov.30	Nov.30	Nov.30	Nov.30	Nov.30	Nov.30	Dec. 1†
Dec. 21	Dec. 21	Dec. 21	Dec. 22†	Dec. 21*	Dec. 21*	Dec. 21	Dec. 21	Dec. 21	Dec. 21	Dec. 22†
26	26*a*	26	26	26	26	26	26	26*a*	26	26
27	27	27*a*	27	27	27	27	27	27	27*a*	27
28	28	28	28*a*	28	28	28	28	28	28	28*a*
Jan. 25	Jan. 25	Jan. 25	Jan. 25*	Jan. 25	Jan. 25	Jan. 25	Jan. 25	Jan. 25	Jan. 25	Jan. 25*
Feb. 2	Feb. 2	Feb. 2	Feb. 2	Feb. 2*	Feb. 2	Feb. 2	Feb. 2	Feb. 2	Feb. 2	Feb. 2
24	24	24	24	24	25†	24	24	24	24	24
Mar.25	Mar.25	Mar.25	Mar.25	Mar.25	Mar.25	Mar.26†	Mar.25	Mar.25	Mar.25	—
Apr. 25	Apr. 25	Apr. 26†	Apr. 27†	Apr. 28†	Apr. 29†	Apr. 30†	May 2†	May 2†	May 3†	—
May 1	May 1*	May 1	May 1	May 1	May 1	May 1	May 1	May 3†	May 4†	—
Jun. 12†	Jun. 13†	Jun. 14†	Jun. 15†	Jun. 16†	Jun. 17†	Jun. 18†	Jun. 19†	Jun. 11	Jun. 11	—

FOR A LEAP YEAR: Read the column to the *right* of that headed by the date of Easter until March 1; then revert to the column headed by the date on which Easter falls.

(*e*) This column is used until March 1 in a Leap Year in which Easter falls upon April 25.

TABLE III: *HOLY DAYS WITH FIXED DATES WHICH ARE NEVER TRANSFERRED*

The Nativity of Our Lord (Christmas Day)	December 25
The Circumcision of Christ	January 1
The Epiphany	January 6
The Nativity of St. John the Baptist	June 24
St. Peter	June 29
St. James	July 25
The Transfiguration of Our Lord	August 6
St. Bartholomew	August 24
St. Matthew	September 21
St. Michael and All Angels	September 29
St. Luke	October 18
St. Simon and St. Jude	October 28
All Saints	November 1

III · THE MUSIC OF THE CHURCH

§1 The Canticles and Psalms

The feature of the Anglican service most likely to confuse the uninitiated is the chanting: indeed, it seems to present difficulties to many organists, choirmasters and choristers of no little experience and ability, for chanting in the majority of our churches leaves much to be desired.

This lack of excellence may be due to misconception regarding the principles of chanting, ill-founded complacency, or an underrating of the importance and technique of chanting. No other part of the service requires more thought and care: nothing else that the choir sings can do more to enhance or mar its contribution to worship of the church.

Most psalters and chant books, in their prefaces, give some directions as to how the books are to be used. In many cases, however, the editors, presuming a certain knowledge on the part of the choirmaster, make their directions so general that they are of little assistance to the church musician who has little experience or advice to draw upon. For those who feel the need of more information than their chant and service books contain, the not-too-general remarks that follow may prove of some small help.

If the reader will refer to his chant book, or to the section of his hymnal devoted to chants, he will find a number of psalms and canticles headed *Venite exultemus*, *Te Deum laudamus*, *Jubilate Deo*, etc. It matters not which he chooses as an example, for the principles which apply to one psalm or canticle apply to all.

Examining first the chants which will be found above or near the canticle, it will be observed that they consist of seven measures (single chants) or fourteen measures (double chants). The measures are divided by double bars into sections of three and four.

Single chant:

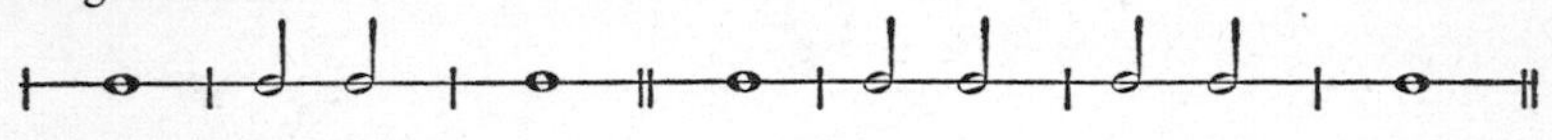

Double chant:

A single chant is sung through once for each verse of the canticle: a double chant serves for two verses. (Occasionally one finds a quadruple chant to which four verses are sung; more rarely, a triple chant which serves for three verses.)

Each verse of the canticle or psalm is divided into small sections by short vertical lines which correspond to the bar lines of the chant. In most psalters a colon or a double vertical line divides the verse into halves and marks the point where the first double bar occurs, and the verse ends with a period or another double vertical line which corresponds to the second double bar in the chant. (Other marks may be used to mark the halves and ends of verses, of course, but whatever marks are used, they are used consistently throughout the psalter.) Each group of words or syllables placed between these vertical lines is sung to one measure of the chant. This device is called *pointing*.

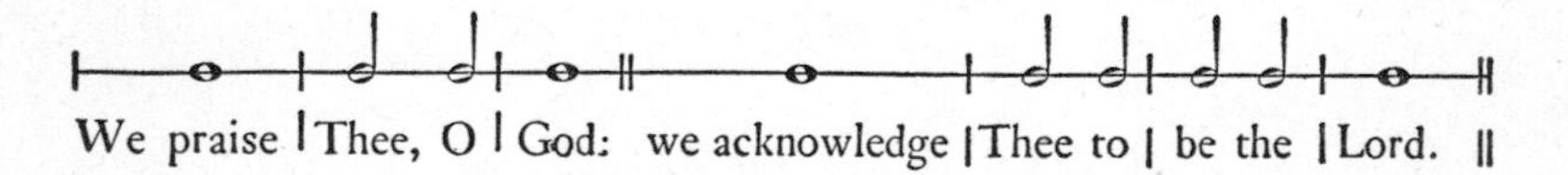

All psalters and service books must agree in the division of the verse into seven groups of syllables, for without such division the words could not be made to conform to the Anglican chant. At this point, however, uniformity ceases, for the methods of breaking up the verse into sections to agree with the measures of the chant are many and varied.

There are two general styles of pointing which, for want of better names, we shall call *singing* and *chanting*.

The *singing* method, which has been widely used for half a century or more, demands that the chants be sung in as nearly strict time as circumstances permit; in other words, the text is subordinated to the measured rhythm of the chant.

The first note of each section of the chant is known as the *reciting note*, and to it may be allotted any number of syllables. It is, therefore, of indeterminate value; but strict time is counted from the accented or stressed syllable.

When only one syllable occurs in the measure the pointing is simple—it is given two beats.

ánd | Israel | his do-| minion.

Words which precede the accented syllable should be recited at a leisurely pace. Too often they are hurried and confused. The accented syllable requires little if any emphasis.

When Is-ra-el cáme | out of | Egypt:

(The notes over the syllables preceding the accent are not intended to indicate time values. Each syllable receives the same quantity and stress as in ordinary speech. These recitations are the only portions of the verses which may properly be said to be *chanted* when this system is used.)

Frequently the first measure of a section contains two notes.

Áll | sheep and | oxen:

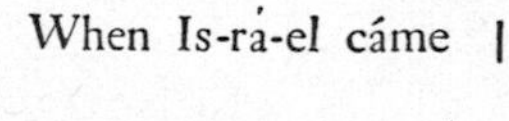

When Is-rá-el cáme | out of | Egypt:

Any syllables which occur after the accent and before the first vertical line should be allotted a fair share of the time in order that they may be enunciated clearly. Many choirs hold the accented syllable too long, to the detriment of what follows.

When two syllables are sung in measured time, the division is usually as follows:

Jú - dah | was his | sanctuary:

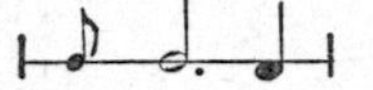

The séa saw | that and | fled:

When three syllables are sung in measured time, the first is usually given one beat, although the three syllables may be sung as triplets.

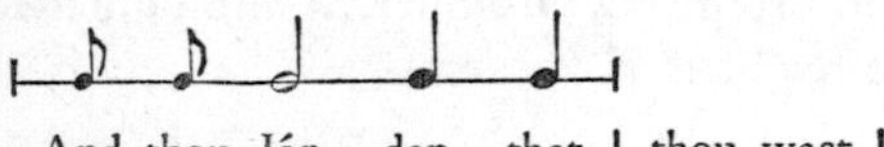

And thou Jór - dan that | thou wast | driven | back.

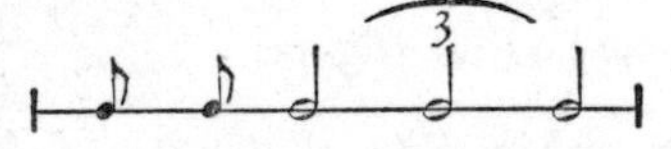

And thou Jór - dan that | thou wast | driven | back.

Or, if the words are to be sung to two notes:

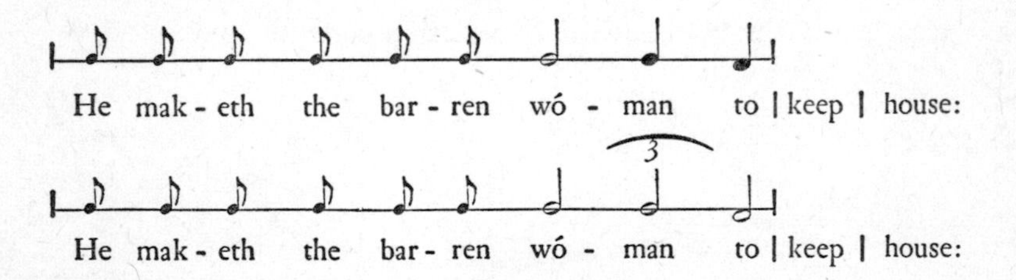

The following should be avoided at all costs:

And thou Jór - dan that | thou wast | driven | back.

He mak - eth the bar - ren wó - man to | keep | house:

When four syllables are to be sung in measured time, they may be of equal value; or, if the syllables following the accent would be passed over lightly in ordinary speech, they may be sung as triplets on the second beat.

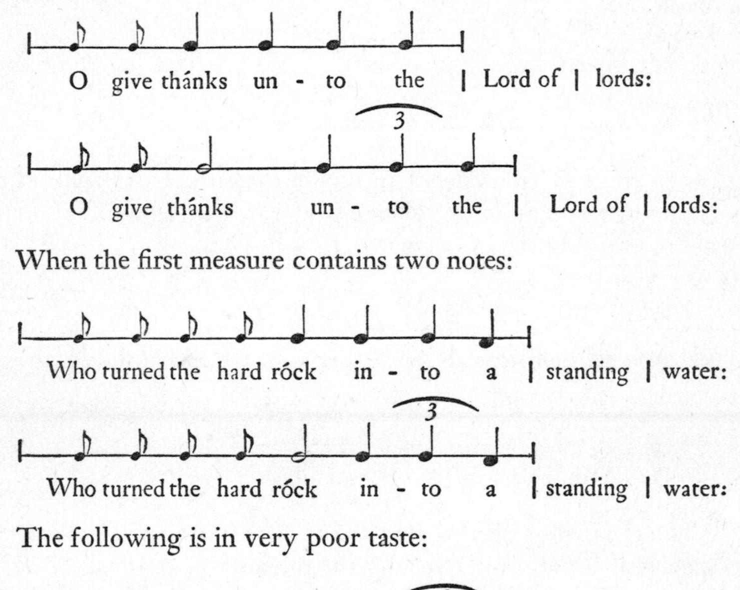

When the first measure contains two notes:

The following is in very poor taste:

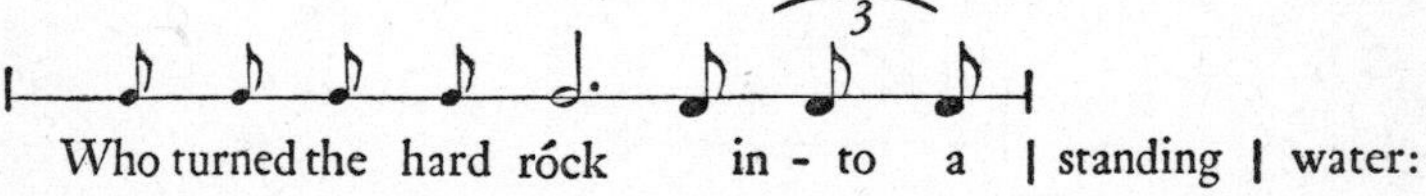

An asterisk indicates a distinct break and a slight pause in the music.

Help me, Lord, * for there is not one | godly · man | left:

Commas are observed as in ordinary speech: they should not be made occasions for long pauses or interruptions.

The measures which normally contain two notes (the second, fifth and sixth, and the corresponding measures in the second part of a double chant) are more often than not required to be sung to two syllables. In such cases, or when only one syllable is to be sung to such a measure, the matching of the words with the notes is simple.

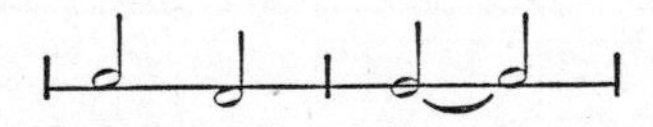

And the house of Jacob from a-| mong the | strange | people.

When three syllables occur in such a measure, their division to correspond to the notes is indicated by a dot or, if the division is between two syllables of one word, by a hyphen.

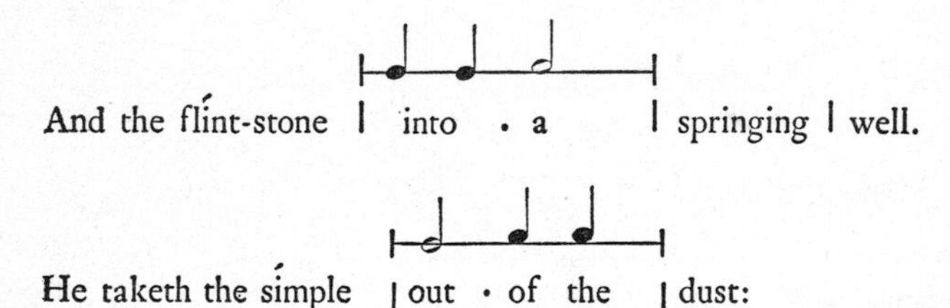

When the first of the three syllables is one that would be stressed in speech, it is permissible to sing the measure in triplets.

and his | glory · a -| bove the | heavens.

Occasionally the two notes of the measure are not of equal value.

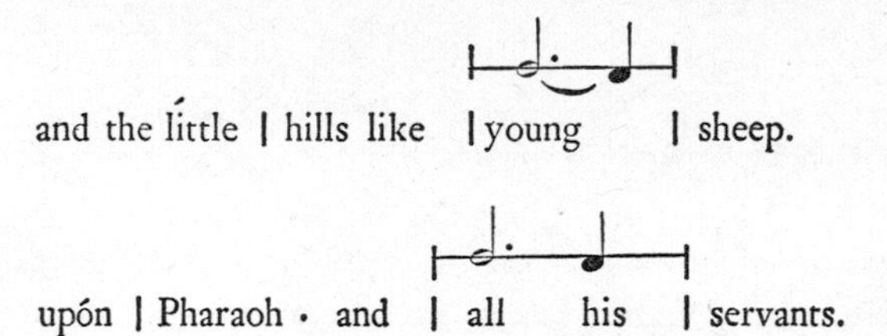

When the second syllable is one that would be stressed slightly in ordinary speech, it may be advisable to sing it on the second beat, borrowing part of the value of the first note.

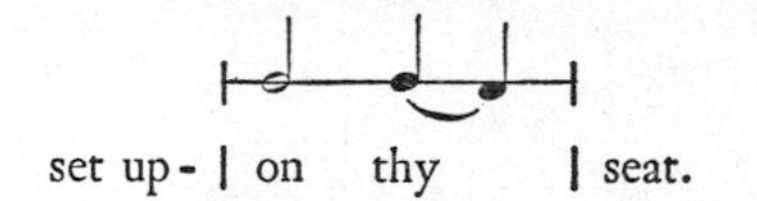

When three syllables occur in such a measure and two are sung to the first note, it may occasionally be preferable to sing them thus:

rather than to syncopate them, thus:

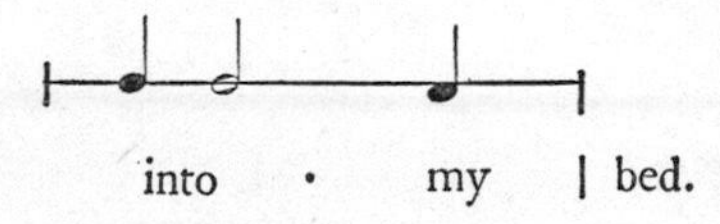

A measure that normally contains two notes may contain three or four, grouped as follows:

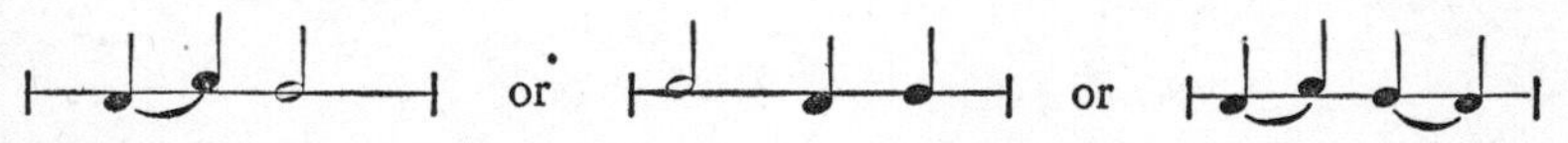

The division of the syllables remains unchanged. Triplets are, of course, impracticable.

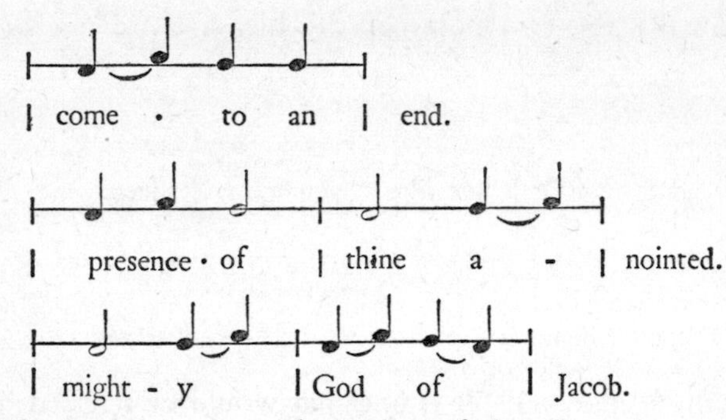

The final measure in each section of the chant (preceding the double bar) more often than not contains only one note.

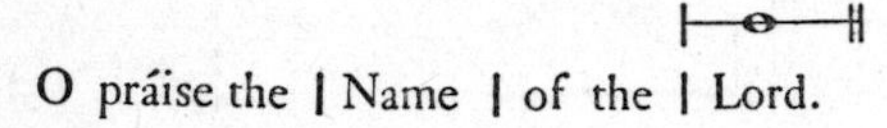

O práise the | Name | of the | Lord.

Práise the | Lord, ye | ser-vants:

until he sée his de- | sire up- | on his | en-em-ies.

Frequently, however, two notes are to be found in the final measure of a half verse, and the division into two distinct beats must be observed.

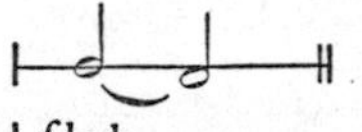

The séa saw | that and | fled:

When Israel cáme | out of | E-gypt:

until he sée his de- | sire up- | on his | enem-ies.

Júdah | was his | sanctu-ary:

When a verse is short, one syllable is often carried through part or all of another measure, the extra beats allotted to it being indicated by dashes.

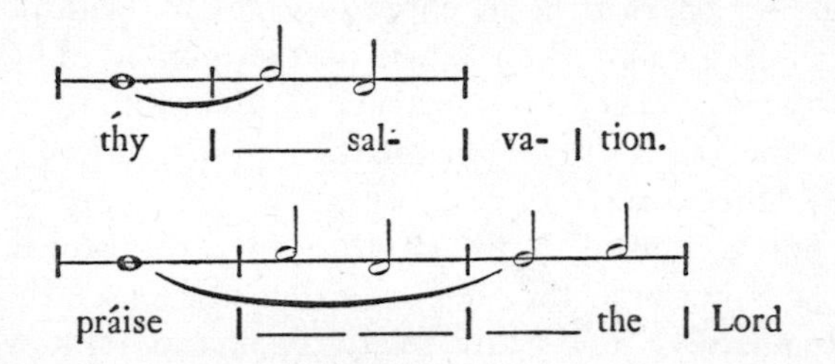

It should be noted that the suffix *-ed* at the end of verbs is, in this method, treated as a separate syllable except when it occurs in the recitation *before* the accent.

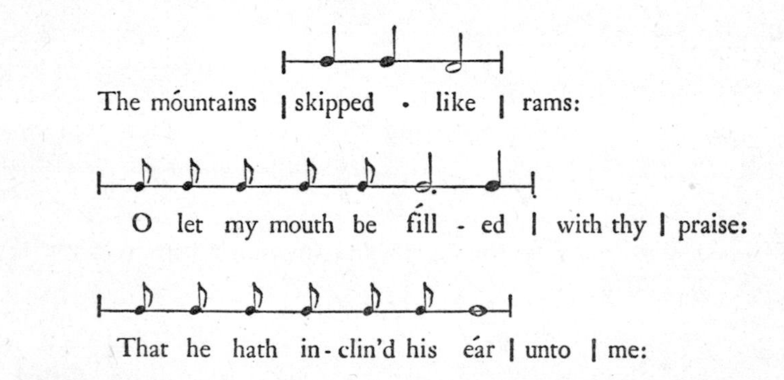

Words such as *blessed*, *planted*, *melted*, *wicked*, etc., in which the suffix is sounded as a separate syllable in ordinary speech, are so treated whether they occur before the accent or not.

Bless-ed be the Lórd | God of | Israel:

The hills melt-ed like wax * at the prés - ence | of the | Lord:

There are probably choirs which, as the result of careful instruction and frequent practice, *sing* the psalms and canticles well. That the syllables before and immediately after the accents are often too hurried, that the accented syllables are held too long and overemphasized cannot be blamed on the method. These are the faults of the singers and their instructors. Actually, the recitations, especially the longer ones, offer the best opportunities for a natural delivery of the words.

It cannot be denied, however, that once the accent has been reached and measured time begins, the utterance of the words is stiff and unnatural. Too many relatively unimportant words such as *and*, *for*, *into* and *upon* occur on the strong beats and assume undue significance, while other syllables that merit stress become secondary.

In spite of good resolutions to pass lightly over prepositions and conjunctions, it is difficult to do so when they fall upon strong first beats; and it is equally difficult to stress important syllables that occur in the last half of a measure. Read aloud the first four verses of the Magnificat, stressing the syllables which will inevitably be stressed when the verses are sung, and notice how unnatural they sound.

1. My soul doth mágnifý the Lórd: and my spirit háth rejóiced in Gód my Sáviour.
2. Fór he háth regárded: the lówliness óf his hánd-máiden.
3. Fór behóld from hénceforth: áll generátions shall cáll me bléssed.
4. For he that is míghty hath mágnified mé: ánd hóly ís his Náme.

If in spite of these objections the choirmaster chooses to have his choir *sing* the canticles and psalms, he will be in good company, for many eminent church musicians continue to use this method. It is to be hoped, however, that the warnings set forth here may help him to achieve better results than those usually heard.

Chanting is an accurate description of a style of rendering the psalms and canticles that is growing in favor. Although newer terms, such as *free rhythm* and *speech rhythm*, are often applied to this method, it is by no means something new, but rather a revival of the old principles of true chanting.

Although the chants are still divided into measures and the words are correspondingly grouped, these divisions have no bearing on the time required to utter the words. Neither have the notes any time value, but are to be regarded merely as indications of pitch. Each syllable is given the same quantity and stress as it would receive in ordinary speech.

The best way to prepare a psalm is to read each verse through naturally at a somewhat leisurely pace; read it through again on a monotone (preferably the first note of the chant); read it a third time, allowing the voice to rise and fall as indicated by the notes of the chant. It is as simple as that!

The cardinal rule, which cannot be too often repeated, is: FORGET TIME VALUES. The printed notes and bar lines have no bearing on the duration of time or on stress. The notes indicate pitch and *nothing else;* the bar lines are conveniences for grouping certain syllables to correspond to certain notes—*they do not measure the time.*

The reciting note may be quite long if it is used for a number of syllables; or it may be very short if only one syllable is placed before the first vertical line and that syllable is a preposition or conjunction.

The divisions of the chant which normally contain two notes (we must not call them *measures* in chanting) may also be short or prolonged, depending upon the number of syllables involved. When there is only one syllable (a circumstance which the newer psalters try to avoid) both notes will have to be chanted, but the syllable should not be unduly prolonged. When the division contains two notes of the same pitch and only one syllable, the syllable must nevertheless be prolonged slightly for the convenience of other choristers whose parts may contain two notes.

When the division of the chant contains more than two notes

no account is taken of the various types of notes; they are made to conform to the words in the same manner as in the *singing* method. When more than two syllables appear in a group, a dot shows their division to correspond to the notes. (Remember that only *pitch*, not *time*, is involved.) Chants which have more than two notes to a division are better avoided when a psalm does not include groupings of more than two syllables.

Some psalters use the numeral 3 to indicate groups of syllables to be chanted as triplets. These may be helpful in some instances, but they serve to introduce the *time* element with which chanters have no concern. Good chanting will take these groups into consideration as a matter of course, and the numeral might conceivably result in inexperienced choristers adopting a certain rigidity of time which would otherwise be avoided.

The last division of each section of the chant (that immediately preceding a double bar) is likewise flexible. The last syllable of a verse or half verse is generally prolonged very slightly. But if in ordinary speech no pause or prolongation would be made between the two halves of a verse, no pause should be observed in chanting, the note before the double bar being shortened to meet the needs of the words.

Although it is risky to attempt writing syllable quantities in notes which are associated with time values, two examples are set forth below. The eighth notes (quavers) represent the quantities that the syllables would receive in ordinary speech: the accent marks suggest normal stress.

For the first example (part of the Magnificat) let us suppose that the notes of the chant are as follows:

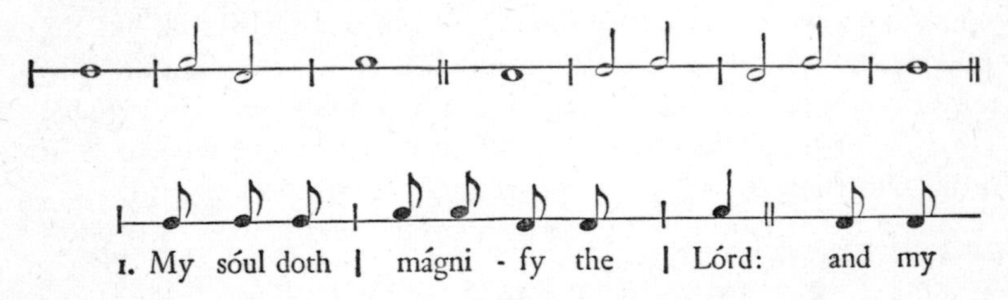

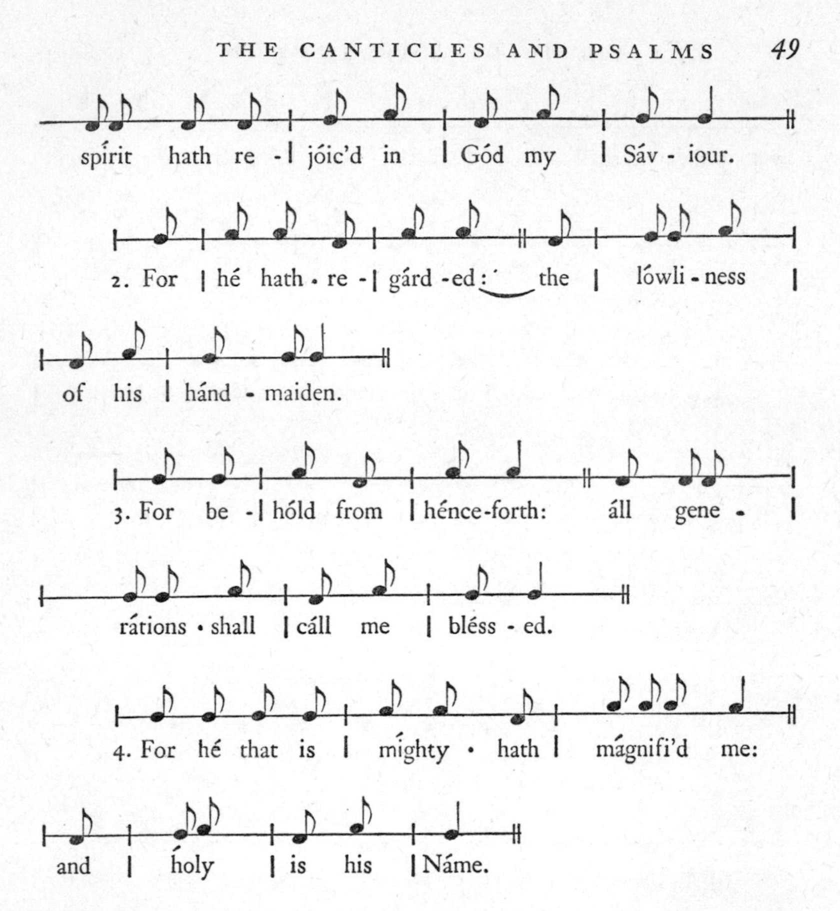

For the second example (part of Psalm XXVII) we shall presume the following arrangement of the notes of a double chant:

1. The Lórd is my líght and my sal - vá - tion; *

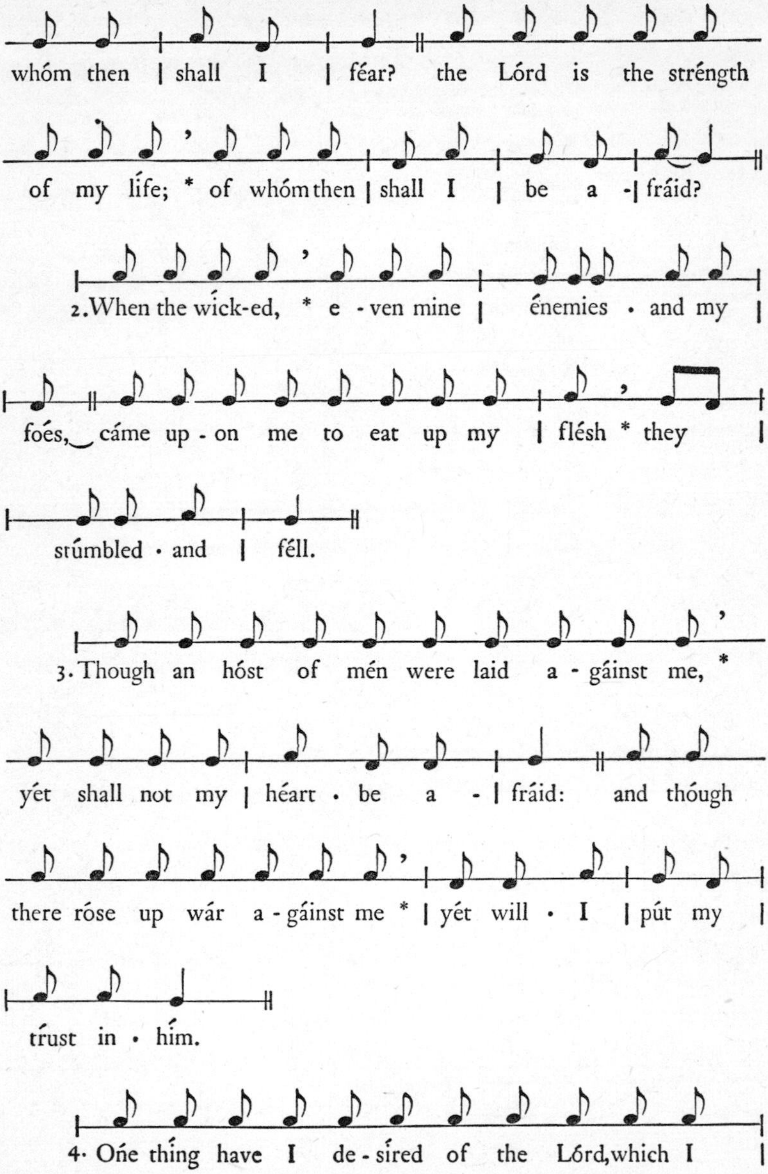

whóm then | shall I | féar? the Lórd is the stréngth

of my lífe; * of whóm then | shall I | be a -| fráid?

2. When the wíck-ed, * e - ven mine | énemies · and my |

foés,‿ cáme up - on me to eat up my | flésh * they |

stúmbled · and | féll.

3. Though an hóst of mén were laid a - gáinst me, *

yét shall not my | héart · be a - | fráid: and thóugh

there róse up wár a - gáinst me * | yét will · I | pút my |

trúst in · hím.

4. Oné thíng have I de - síred of the Lórd, which I |

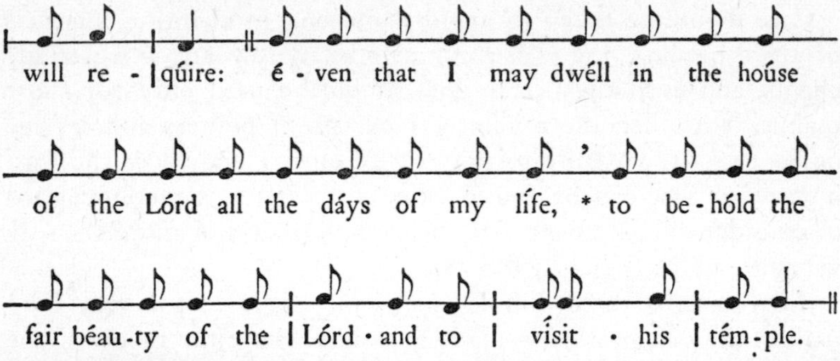

will re - | qúire: é - ven that I may dwéll in the hoúse

of the Lórd all the dáys of my lífe, * to be - hóld the

fair béau - ty of the | Lórd · and to | vísit · his | tém - ple.

The natural, unhurried flow of words in *chanting*, the ease with which ugly emphases are avoided and desirable stresses observed, will appeal to all who have regard for the beauty of expression of the English language.

One of the happiest features of chanting is its simplicity. A choir accustomed to *singing* the canticles and psalms may find it a little difficult to abandon old habits, but even inexperienced singers will quickly grasp the principles of chanting and acquire the ability to chant easily and well.

It is possible, but not advisable, to *chant* canticles and psalms to pointing that has been designed for *singing*. Better results are obtained with the use of a psalter pointed for chanting. In some of the newer psalters a strong syllable is placed immediately after each vertical line, so that a choir yielding to the temptation to stress the first note of a measure will do no violence to the sense of the words.

While any Anglican chant may be used for any canticle or psalm (whether sung or chanted) the choirmaster will do well to exercise judgement in his choice of chants. A penitential psalm requires a chant in serious mood, perhaps in a minor key; a quiet, meditative psalm (such as the twenty-third) need not be grave, but it should be chanted quietly; while a bright psalm or the Te Deum will demand a bright chant. Some chants are traditionally associated with certain psalms, but a choirmaster need not feel bound to use a chant set for a particular psalm if, in his opinion, another chant is more suitable.

Care should be taken to avoid monotony in chanting. Because of their brevity, there are comparatively few attractive single chants, and even the better ones should be used only for short psalms. It has become a habit for editors of psalters and service books to set the Venite to only single chants, and those the least interesting that can be found. The choirmaster is recommended to consider double chants for this and all psalms of more than six verses.

Two or even three double chants may be used for very long psalms, the changes being made at points where the mood of the psalm changes slightly. A quadruple chant is useful for long psalms. If the number of verses is uneven, the second half of a double chant is repeated either for the last verse or for some other verse indicated in the psalter.

There is no reason for not using double chants for short psalms, although one would scarcely go so far as to use a quadruple chant for four or eight verses.

It is well to provide some variety in the music for the canticles and psalms. There is no more justification for using the same chants Sunday after Sunday than there would be for repeating the same hymn tunes and anthems. A choir that chants the canticles and psalms at Morning and Evening Prayer on Sundays only should know at least forty chants.

The psalms are often chanted antiphonally, one side of the choir (traditionally the south side) taking the first verse, the other side responding with the second verse. Certain verses (indicated in most psalters) and the Gloria Patri are chanted by the whole choir.

Antiphonal chanting requires choristers from each of the four parts on both sides of the choir. However, even with small choirs which seat all the sopranos and tenors on one side, and all the altos and basses on the other, antiphonal chanting is possible to a limited degree. It will be necessary to choose chants which are suitable for unison chanting, and it should not be continued for long unless the organist is skillful in varying the accompaniment.

It is sometimes effective to have the men chant one verse in unison and the boys (or women) the next, but this should not be repeated too often.

In a long psalm, some variety may be obtained by using a descant occasionally. Descants for chants are rarely heard (few have been written, in fact) but there is no good reason for not using them. (Descants will be discussed more fully in the section on "Hymns.")

Thus far, we have dealt only with Anglican chants, which conform to the pattern of seven measures for a single and fourteen measures for a double chant. Mention must here be made of the Gregorian or plainsong chant which, although not nearly as popular as the Anglican chant, is worthy of serious consideration and study.

The Gregorian chant varies in form, but the grouping of syllables to match the notes is generally clearly indicated. The notes are indications of pitch only, and have no time value. Their duration depends upon the time required to utter the syllables that go with them. The words are chanted at a natural, unhurried pace, syllables being prolonged slightly only when chanted to more than one note. All that has been said about quantity and stress in regard to *chanting* Anglican chants applies with equal force to the Gregorian chant.

Each chant begins with an Intonation (consisting generally of two or three notes) which is used only for the first verse and the Gloria Patri. The first half of the first verse is chanted by the priest or precentor alone, without accompaniment; the second half is chanted by the full choir with the organ. Thereafter, the canticle or psalm is preferably chanted antiphonally, the section of the choir on the south side taking the even verses, and the north side taking the odd ones. The Gloria Patri and any verses marked "Full" are, of course, chanted by the whole choir.

Gregorian chants may be in harmony, but a grander effect is produced when they are in unison. Thus chanted, with a varied and skillful organ accompaniment, they have a beauty unlike any other music.

The Gregorian chant is mentioned only briefly here for two reasons: first, because its use is so limited that comparatively few student choirmasters will find need for it; but chiefly because it would be presumptuous on the part of the writer of this book to enlarge upon a subject which has been treated by far more capable writers. Plainsong is a specialized branch of church music, and he who would practise it would do well to seek expert tuition. If the choirmaster has any doubt concerning his knowledge or comprehension of plainsong, he would better leave it alone, for it is too beautiful to be marred by the unskilled.

There is a great need for general improvement in chanting, and the village choirmaster can (and often does) come nearer to perfection than many of his colleagues in large city churches. It is a grave mistake to hurry over the preparation of the psalms in order to get at the anthem. Any choir can sing an anthem reasonably well: very few choirs can chant.

§2 The Versicles and Responses

It is traditional in the Anglican church to sing, chant or intone at least some of the prayers and responses.

The custom was, primarily, one of convenience. A clergyman taking service in a large church can more easily make himself heard by raising the pitch of his voice than he could by forcing his natural speech: the congregation, responding in like manner, will utter their words more distinctly, in contrast to the unintelligible mutterings so often heard when the responses are "said."

Since the natural inflections of the voice are not easily achieved under such circumstances, artificial and sometimes elaborate inflections have been invented. The responses have thus become an embellishment to the service, and the original reason for intoning them is generally overlooked. Those who object to the intoning of the responses do so because they regard intoning purely as an embellishment; and in small churches where the natural speaking pitch would be sufficient to carry the voice to all the congregation, intoning may truly be more of an embellishment than anything else, since it has not the same utilitarian purpose that it has in larger churches. But whatever the motive, intoning is firmly established in the Anglican tradition, and should be encouraged as a normal mode of expression rather than something special that tends to confuse the congregation on festivals.

Two sets of responses for Morning and Evening Prayer are in general use: the *Ferial* and the *Festal*. In their original forms they begin with the responses after the first Lord's Prayer and end with the Third Collect. In many churches, only the part of the service between those two points is intoned, that having comprised the entire service of Morning and Evening Prayer at the time the music for the responses was provided.

Although traditionalists are very touchy upon the subject, it must be declared that the argument for intoning or chanting only part of the service is deficient in logic. Since the Prayer Book itself has undergone revision, surely the music that accompanies it is not too sacred for similar revision at the hands of competent church musicians. (Indeed, this work has been done; although the music has not been so much revised as edited and extended to meet the needs of the longer service.) Would those who insist that only the parts of the service known to Tallis should be intoned, ask the Canadian and American churches to interrupt a sung Litany to say, in the natural voice, those petitions that were not in the early English Prayer Book?

It seems far more consistent, and certainly it is in quite good form, to intone the entire service or to intone none of it. However, every point of view must be respected, and all usages will be taken into consideration when the various services of the church are being discussed.

The Ferial setting of the responses is more suited to choirs which *chant* and, while the name suggests its use only for services other than festivals, it may well be used on all occasions.

The manner in which the responses are chanted often depends

upon the system of notation employed. Some choirs forget that the notes are not intended to represent time values. The following version is not intended to be sung in strict time, despite the notation:

Usually one chord of indeterminate value is given for all but the last two syllables, and the words are monotoned with the same quantities and stresses as in normal speech.

It will be noticed that, because the alto has two notes for one syllable, this and the last syllable must be prolonged. To be consistent, the prolongation of the last two syllables must occur even when there is no real necessity for it:

If the unnatural prolongations are to be avoided, it is desirable to use a version which omits the C sharp in the alto. The entire response may then be made naturally.

The priest should be prevailed upon to practise with the choir occasionally in order that his manner of intoning may agree with that of the choir.

The responses, like the canticles and psalms, should be chanted at an easy, unhurried pace, but without unnatural drawling.

The Festal responses must be *sung*. Some slight modifications may be made to relieve the stiffness of strict time, but true chanting cannot be achieved.

The tempo of the Festal setting must be left to the discretion of the choirmaster. One is tempted to recommend a "dignified pace," but ideas of dignity vary so widely that the recommendation is meaningless. Generally speaking, the responses may be sung fairly briskly in a small church, but more slowly in a large building.

In some churches where daily services are held, the Festal Responses are used on Sundays and Red Letter Days, the Ferial setting on week days. Where services are held only on Sundays, the Ferial setting is often used except on major festivals. But it is not improper to use the Ferial Responses at any time; and when it is desired to adhere to the *chanting* method, the Festal setting may be disregarded altogether.

While it is unusual to depart from the traditional settings of the responses, other settings do exist and may well be used if they seem especially suited to the needs of a particular congregation.

Any convenient note may be given to the clergyman for intoning the prayers. The custom is to play the *Amen* after all intoned prayers, and to play a soft accompaniment for all parts of the service which are intoned by the whole congregation. An organist who is not confident of his ability to improvise a background for the intoned parts of the service will have no difficulty in securing accompaniments.

§3 The Hymns

Hymns used in the Anglican service are, as a rule, dignified in character. There is no place for verses which are frankly sentimental, those in which a line is repeated over and over as a refrain, Negro spirituals and "gospel" hymns. If this statement seems to reflect a superior attitude, let us hasten to say that no Anglican disparages the spiritual or inspirational values of a type of church music used by large numbers of sincere Christian people. It is not used in the Anglican church for the same reason that a plainsong tune would not be used at a revival meeting—it is out of place.

The choirmaster might expect that any hymn contained in the official hymnals of the church could be used without question or examination. Unfortunately, this is not the case. The committees that compile these books are sometimes caught nodding; sometimes, indeed, a committee will surrender a complete section of a hymnal to a very poor type of hymn which they believe to be suitable for Sunday Schools or mission services.

Most people are indifferent to the words they sing in church. Even those who are critical of the verse they read throw all literary standards to the winds where hymns are concerned. Yet, as the church in its liturgy so carefully preserves the beautiful and dignified phraseology of the Bible and the early Prayer Book, as the preacher is expected to express his thoughts lucidly, logically and in the language of a scholar, surely it is not too much to ask that our hymns possess some literary merit.

The tests of a good hymn are the tests of any piece of poetry.

It is not suggested, of course, that any good poem can be considered suitable for use as a hymn; but, certainly, any hymn should be good poetry. While the responsibility for the hymns that are to be sung is generally assumed by the rector, the choirmaster should take a firm stand in support of good hymns, and be prepared to choose them discriminately if and when he is called upon to do so. For no music, however worthy, can compensate for poor words.

If hymns should be good poetry, hymn tunes should certainly be good music. Tastes in music, as in poetry, vary; but, while neither is subject to strict specifications, there are recognized standards of excellence. Tunes by Crüger, Filitz, Bourgeois, Gibbons, Tallis, Croft, Dykes, Stainer and Vaughan Williams are representative of several schools and periods that have stood the test of time. They might well be consulted by young musicians who feel the need for bases of comparison when estimating the worth of other composers, periods and styles of church music.

Plainsong tunes, well sung and accompanied, have a peculiar beauty. They can be made effective even by small choirs and, since they are sung in unison, may solve the problem of a choirmaster who cannot muster four parts. Good chanting that teaches the choir to disregard measured time, bar lines and strong beats is excellent preparation for plainsong.

A choirmaster who has had no experience with plainsong would be wise not to attempt it without first seeking instruction, written or oral, from one who specializes in that type of music. There are several books on the subject, and most lovers of the art are enthusiasts who would gladly lend assistance to a convert!

Plainsong is not widely used, and it must be admitted that it seldom appeals to ears that are not accustomed to it. In a parish where it has not been used, it should be introduced cautiously and in small doses. An entire service in plainsong might be the ideal of the choirmaster, but it would be resented by a congregation that had never heard plainsong. The same caution should be exercised in introducing any style of music strange to the choir or congregation, lest the choirmaster defeat his own purpose by impatience.

For many hymns, the hymnals offer a choice of more than one tune. In making his decision, the choirmaster should consider musical merit first. If two tunes are of equal worth, preference may be given to one which has long been used in the parish: if neither is good, an alternative tune may be chosen.

The metres (indicating the number of syllables to a line) are generally printed above the tunes; for example, 6.6.6.6. shows that the tune was written for a four-line verse and that each line must contain six syllables. In some cases, letters are used: C.M. for Common Metre is substituted for 8.6.8.6., L.M. for Long Metre is 8.8.8.8., S.M. for Short Metre is 6.6.8.6. The letter *D* (for *double*) in D.C.M., D.L.M., D.S.M., 7.6.7.6.D., etc., shows that the verse is of eight lines, and that the last half of the verse has the same syllable pattern as the first half.

The metrical marks and the metrical index near the back of the hymnal, while of great assistance when substitute tunes are being sought, are not infallible guides. One could not, for instance, use the same tune for both the following hymns, although both are marked 7.6.7.6.D.—

Come, ye faithful, raise the strain
 Of triumphant gladness;
God hath brought his Israel
 Into joy from sadness; *etc.*

O Word of God Incarnate,
 O Wisdom from on high,
O Truth unchanged, unchanging,
 O Light of our dark sky. *etc.*

The first requires a tune that begins on a strong first beat; the second demands an anticipatory beat in order that the strong first beats of the measures may coincide with the stressed syllables. In a few books, the metrical index divides, where necessary, tunes having the same metre; those with a strong first syllable being listed as *Trochaic*, those with a weak first syllable as *Iambic*. This classification is by no means generally observed by compilers of hymnals; and when it is not, the choirmaster must exercise some caution.

It is important that the character of the tune should be appropriate to the thoughts expressed by the words. No person of good judgement would consider the tune for

> Forty days and forty nights
> Thou wast fasting in the wild; *etc.*

interchangeable with that for

> Praise, O praise our God and King,
> Hymns of adoration sing; *etc.*

although no metrical difficulties would be encountered. Nevertheless, tunes are often selected which are not consistent with the spirit of the words and, as a result, the effectiveness of the hymns is lessened. Vigilance and discrimination are necessary not only in the selection of substitute tunes, but also in considering the tunes which the hymnal "sets" for certain hymns, for the judgement of compiling committees is not invariably unerring. If it seems desirable, the choirmaster need not hesitate to use tunes not contained in the hymnal.

The use of alternative tunes can be carried too far, of course. While, as has been said, compiling committees do err, they do not err consistently; and before discarding a tune of their choice, the choirmaster should weigh carefully his reasons for doing so against the committee's reasons for prescribing the tune. The fact that a tune is new to the choirmaster or to the parish is not sufficient grounds for rejection. All tunes which are now popular were once new, and our hymnals contain many tunes that might become popular if choirmasters would teach them to their choirs and congregations. The habit of using only a few tunes and substituting them whenever possible cannot be too strongly condemned. Such tunes as *Aurelia, Winchester Old, Regent Square, St. George,* and *Martyrdom,* splendid though they are, should not be sung two or three times a month to a variety of hymns which have other good tunes set to them.

Having decided that a tune has musical merit, that the metre is correct, and that it reflects the mood of the hymn, one should make sure that it will not interfere with the easy phrasing of the words.

Phrasing does not receive the attention it deserves. The whole meaning of a verse may be lost or distorted by taking breaths in the wrong places or failing to take them in the right ones. The pernicious habit of making a break at the end of every line and in the middle of long ones is a certain sign that the choir and people have little interest in what they are singing. It is a sheer waste of time to make a careful choice of hymns that are to be sung in such a manner.

More often than not, certain lines from the hymn, "For all the saints," are sung as if they were punctuated as follows:

For all the saints who, from their labors rest,

Thou in the darkness, drear their one true light.

Yet all are one in, thee for all are thine.

And when the strife is, fierce the warfare long,

And hearts are brave a-, gain and arms are strong.

Sweet is the calm of, Paradise the blest.

Here are a few familiar examples from other hymns:

Room to deny ourselves a road,
To lead us daily nearer God.

Thy kingdom come on bended knee,
The passing ages pray.

I have no help but, thine nor do I need,
Another arm save, thine to lean upon.

If with honest hearted,
Love for God and man.

Hark how the heavenly anthem drowns,
All music but its own.

O come thou Rod of Jesse free,
Thine own from Satan's tyranny.

These examples are not given in an attempt to be funny or to exaggerate. They are quite commonplace, and pages could be filled with similar examples. And they are—or should be—as offensive to the ear that hears them sung as to the eye that reads them in print.

Choirs should be trained to take breaths where punctuation marks occur. As a rule this is not difficult if the singers form the habit of taking a few deep breaths in a stanza instead of shallow gasps every two or three measures.

It is not suggested that a long phrase or sentence be sung in one breath even if it leaves the choir in a state of exhaustion. There are instances where it would be extremely difficult to sing from punctuation mark to punctuation mark without taking a breath. However, even in such cases the sense of the words can be preserved by making breaks only at the beginnings or endings of subordinate clauses or phrases.

The following probably would not be sung in one breath by the choir, certainly not by the congregation:

If on our daily course our mind
Be set to hallow all we find;

but there would be no objection to imagining a comma after "course" and taking a breath there.

Or in the following, which is not easily sung in two breaths by untrained singers:

Bright the vision that delighted
Once the sight of Judah's seer;
Sweet the countless tongues united
To entrance the prophet's ear.

There could be no serious objection to taking breaths after "vision" and "tongues"—certainly it would be preferable to taking breaths at the ends of the lines.

Most phrasing difficulties melt away with a little forethought. The principal thing is to pre-determine where breaths are to be taken when punctuation marks are few and far between. These extra breathing places may be marked, but the choir will be more alert if they are expected to remember such details.

The breaking up of phrases that should not be broken up is not the only fault of the one-line-equals-one-breath method of singing hymns: it frequently results in running together phrases or words that should be separated. One often hears the words, "Holy, holy, holy," sung as if they were one word of six syllables: "holyholyholy."

Commas and other punctuation marks should be observed. It is not necessary that breaths be taken or the tempo interrupted, but there should be slight cessations of sound.

Occasionally, if the hymn is rather dramatic, the breaks may be slightly exaggerated, but only when they add to the effectiveness of the words. Here are some examples, written as if in prose that the phrasing may be more readily evident:

> The wild winds hushed; the angry deep sank, like a little child, to sleep.

> I heard the voice of Jesus say: "Behold, I freely give the living water, thirsty one. Stoop down, and drink, and live."

> Give me the wings of faith, to rise within the veil, and see the saints above; how great their joys, how bright their glories be.

No other phrasing is practicable, regardless of where the lines of the verses end.

Congregations reflect the habits of their choirs, and will soon notice and imitate new habits in hymn-singing. The organist can do much to help the situation by observing the phrasing: it is not necessary to keep one's fingers glued to the manual throughout each verse.

The tempo of the hymn often makes the difference between good and poor phrasing. A hymn that has many long phrases may well be sung at a brisk tempo; one that has many commas should be taken at a comparatively leisurely pace to allow for the punctuation. There is nothing irreverent in singing hymns fairly quickly, and much is gained if it results in improved phrasing.

Hymn tunes are written as the composers intended them to be sung, and a tune written in four parts generally suffers when it is sung in unison. In some small churches there is a tendency on the part of the choir men (and the clergy) to "sing the air" on the slightest provocation. Although they would not care to admit it, the reason is sheer laziness—it requires less mental effort to sing the melody "by ear" than to read a part.

When representatives of the four parts are present, there is seldom good reason for singing a four-part tune in unison. It must be remembered that the sopranos have the support of the organ and the entire congregation, and the doubtful assistance of the rector and half a dozen choir men will not compensate for the loss of harmony.

In some small churches four parts are not available, and it may be necessary to sing in unison. As far as possible, *tunes written to be sung in unison* should be used, supplemented by four-part tunes whose interest is not too dependent on the harmony. Even so, the tunes should be practised in parts at rehearsals. The church owes its choristers some training in return for their services, and that training should certainly include instruction in the singing of parts.

When a four-part tune is sung in unison, either from necessity or for a special effect, the organist should supply a varied accompaniment to make up in interest what is lost in the voice parts.

But too much stress cannot be laid on the fact that the normal manner of singing hymns is in four parts. The choirmaster should insist upon his altos, tenors and basses singing the notes written for them unless, for some special reason, he gives instructions to the contrary. No man who would refuse to wear his wife's hat in public has a right to sing his wife's part in church.

An interesting variation of the hymn tune is the *faux bourdon*

—loosely, "false melody." Faux bourdons are not new. Their use is the revival of an old form which gave the melody to the tenors. To the sopranos is allotted an independent melodious part, and the altos and basses also have independent parts. As the melody of the hymn should be prominent, the successful use of faux bourdons demands a fairly strong tenor section and a singing congregation. Faux bourdons are not recommended for all churches: the choirmaster should weigh very carefully the chances of success before trying them.

Another variation of the hymn tune, and one that requires fewer resources than the faux bourdon, is the *descant*, an independent melody sung by the sopranos (or some of them) while the other members of the choir sing the melody in unison.

A prerequisite for a voice which is to sing descants is the ability to sing upper G (or a little higher) clearly and easily, for descants are written high. Boys' voices are admirably suited to this purpose for, with any real training, their best register is near the top of and above the treble staff.

The greater the intervals between the notes of the descant and those of the melody, the fewer will be the voices required for the descant—a few boys will do wonders under such an arrangement. When the notes of the descant and the melody are closer together, and when some of the notes of the descant go below the melody, the descant will not stand out as clearly unless more or stronger voices are allotted to it.

When a descant is written without a special accompaniment, the organist must either improvise his own or play the original four-part harmony of the tune. More effective are the descants in which the composers have not felt bound to the original harmonies, but have supplied freer and independent accompaniments.

Descants can be sung satisfactorily even in small parish churches. Boys learn them easily and can soon be taught to sing them well.

Some hymnals contain a few descants and faux bourdons: other excellent arrangements are available from music publishers. Like all good things, they can be overdone: their effectiveness lies in their occasional use as a contrast to the four-part version of the tunes. The congregation should be informed that descants and faux bourdons are not intended to deprive them of opportunities to sing; on the contrary, congregational singing is desirable if not necessary.

Perhaps this would be a good place to mention that sore subject, the processional hymn. It has become the custom in many churches, particularly in Canada and the United States, for the choir to sing the opening hymn while walking in pairs from the entrance of the church to their places in the choir. In some parishes the custom has become so deeply rooted that it would surprise the people to learn that there was any other way of beginning a service.

The only thing that can be said in favor of the processional hymn is that it adds a little pageantry. Well done, it can be impressive; and it is not altogether inappropriate on major church festivals.

One of the chief objections to processionals is that they are so seldom appropriate. The chief services of the church begin on a note of humility, and it is not easy to establish a humble or meditative mood with choristers marching up the aisle. Particularly in penitential seasons it is an irksome task to find hymns which make satisfactory processionals and at the same time reflect the mood of the season.

From the standpoint of the singers, processionals present some difficulty. It is no easy matter to sing and breathe correctly while walking; and, if the procession starts at some distance from the organ, there is a danger of losing the tempo which the organist is trying to maintain. Then, too, the habit of many choirs of singing processionals in unison makes matters worse for altos and basses who have to sing notes above their accustomed range under the most unfavorable conditions. There is no good reason for singing processionals in unison; there are many reasons for not doing so.

It is not supposed that these remarks will cause processionals to be abolished in churches where they have become established (bad habits are ever more persistently clung to than good ones); but it is hoped that choirmasters may be dissuaded from introducing them in churches where they have not been used heretofore.

§4 Anthems

When a choir has learned to sing the hymns, responses, psalms and canticles well, some time may be devoted to the preparation of anthems. Their choice will depend largely upon the musical taste of the choirmaster, and no definite directions can be given for his assistance.

When one remembers the host of musicians who have made fine contributions to the music of the church, it seems unfair to mention any few by name. Nevertheless, for the benefit of any young choirmaster who may feel the need of recommendations, the works of the following are suggested as being representatives of various styles and periods: Tye, Gibbons, Croft, Boyce, Wesley, Stainer, Bairstow, T. T. Noble, Voris, Vaughan Williams, Willan and Thiman. No list of anthems or composers would meet the approval of all church musicians, and the list given here is no exception. Many choirmasters favor certain "schools" of music. A few years ago there was a fad for Russian anthems, some choirs make a specialty of Bach, others sing Tudor music or the moderns almost exclusively.

It has become fashionable in some circles to disdain the works of Victorian composers—Stainer, Woodward, Dykes, etc. It must be remembered, however, that these later nineteenth-century composers made a valuable contribution to church music at a time when there was a great need for singable anthems that were not beyond the capabilities of the average parish choir or the musical understanding of the congregation. They were an important factor in promoting the growth of choirs in small churches.

Some music libraries contain nothing else but Victorian anthems and, while every effort should be made to introduce different styles and to achieve a better balance, one should hesitate before banishing these old favorites. For it must be admitted that the Victorians had a knack of catching the spirit of scriptural texts and clothing them with music that seems a part of them. When we hear read as part of the lesson, "What are these that are arrayed in white robes? and whence came they?" or "I am Alpha and Omega," we can easily imagine Stainer sitting beside St. John and writing down the notes as the evangelist penned the words! After all, the anthem must help the people in their devotions, and if the Victorians accomplish this end better than the impersonal, austere moderns, then the Victorians should remain the mainstay of the choir until newer (or older) idioms become more familiar and appreciated.

No anthem should be sung merely because it was written by a famous musician: many good composers occasionally wrote below their usual standard, and such masters as Mozart, Beethoven and Brahms left very little that is of use to the parish choir.

On the other hand, an anthem need not be passed over because it was written by an obscure composer. Much fine music has been written by men who gained little notice.

In short, each anthem should be judged by its merits—its musical value, the suitability of the words, and its practicability from the standpoint of the choristers who are to sing it.

In regard to the words: the choirmaster is quite safe in choosing anthems whose texts are contained in the Bible, the Prayer Book, or the official hymnal. (The American Prayer Book contains a note to this effect.) When other words form the subject of an anthem, the approval of the rector should be sought. There are many anthems from old services and liturgies (such as the prayers beginning "Save us, O Lord, waking; guard us sleeping" and "O Lord, support us all the day long") and others based on inspired poems (such as Longfellow's "As torrents in summer" from *King Olaf*, and "O gladsome light" from *The Golden Legend*) that rectors will be glad to approve. Anthems which lack dignity and inspiration are better avoided.

Extended forms of the canticles ("service settings" as they are sometimes called) are judged as anthems—which, indeed, they are. There is a difference of opinion as to the use of these longer, more elaborate settings. Some argue that, in using them rather than chants, the congregation is prevented from joining in a part of the service which they should sing. There is much merit in this argument, for congregational singing should be encouraged. Nevertheless, longer settings are frequently used, and may be sung in place of anthems if the choirmaster does not wish to rob the people of their chants. On occasions of rejoicing the Te Deum is often used as an anthem at an evening service or at a communion service—not at Morning Prayer, of course, for there it is properly sung after the first lesson.

The standards which are applied to anthems are applied also to complete settings of the Communion Service, which may be quite simple or (especially the Creed and the Gloria in Excelsis) fairly elaborate.

It is wise to keep the music within the capabilities of the choir. Nothing is more discouraging than to work hard on a too-difficult anthem or service and to sing it, eventually, in a manner that falls short of the composer's intention.

On the other hand, the choir's ability should be extended; and it is helpful to have in practice an anthem which taxes their skill but which is not impossible of performance. Choirs respond quickly to such a challenge. A programme of progress is beneficial to both the choir and the music of the church.

Where singers for four parts are available, the supply of anthems is almost without limit; but even if four parts are not represented some attempt should be made to learn music apart from the hymns, canticles, etc. Anthems are obtainable for various combinations of voices. Soprano and alto arrangements may be found useful, any men present being assigned the part for which their voices are best suited; two-soprano settings (air and descant) may also be used, the men joining in the melody.

Unison songs with independent organ accompaniments are always good. (The objections to unison singing do not, of course, apply to compositions written to be sung in unison.)

What has been said about the selection of anthems applies also to solos, duets, etc. The frequent use of solos is not recommended. There are few soloists who have the knack of self-effacement, and anything in the service which attracts the attention of the people towards an individual falls short of the devotional ideal. Furthermore, apart from the oratorios, there are very few solos which measure up to the church's standard of music. Perhaps ninety per cent of the "sacred solos" might be described as ballads with sacred words (some have not even that saving feature) and the accompaniments are totally unsuited to the organ.

§5 Organ Music

Organists are, as a rule, fairly well acquainted with the music of their instrument, and it would be presumptuous to attempt more than a few general remarks in a manual of this kind.

It may be well to mention that some music which might be acceptable in some other churches is not considered appropriate in the Anglican church. The purpose of an Anglican organist is not to amuse and entertain, but rather to establish and maintain the note of reverence which should prevail throughout the service. Only by playing good music can he achieve this purpose.

What constitutes good music, and what good music is suitable for a church service are matters on which there is a diversity of opinion; and the organist will have to rely largely upon his training, his musical background, and his sense of the fitness of things. Much organ music has been written with the church in mind, but this is, in itself, no guarantee of its suitability.

Obviously, music that is light and frivolous, or in a rhythm more likely to excite than to calm, must be ruled out. However, it need not be dull. One of the objections to much of the music that has been handed down to us from the Victorian era is that it has no life—nothing for the ear to fasten upon or the memory to retain. There are hundreds of such pieces, good music insofar as they are correctly harmonized, but lacking the power to entice minds from the distracting sights and sounds that are often present before a service.

Somewhere between the frivolous and the dull, then, the organist must choose his music, and his field is by no means a small one.

There exists a school of organists who would rather perish than play anything melodious that might appeal to the ear of a layman. But it is to the layman's ear that the organist must appeal and, while there is no need to lower one's musical standards, some concessions should be made to the layman's lack of appreciation of profound music. Such pieces as Bach's *Jesu, Joy of Man's Desiring* and the Air from Samuel Wesley's *Three Short Pieces* might be cited as examples of music that should satisfy the organist's standards, arouse the interest of the congregation and, used as voluntaries, create an atmosphere conducive to worship. The slower movements from some of the organ sonatas also make excellent voluntaries—the Guilmant C minor, the Rheinberger C minor, and the Mendelssohn No. 1 for examples.

What has been said about Victorian organ music should not be construed as a blanket condemnation. Not all of it is dull, and some of it is admirable. The works of Batiste and Guilmant, while very much out of fashion these days, have much to offer the organist who can separate wheat from chaff. If the music fulfills the purpose for which the organist requires it, one need not worry greatly about its origin.

Music for postludes is, as a rule, rather bright, but it need not be confined to noisy marches. A bouree or a fugue or a quieter gavotte may, upon occasion, be preferable to a march.

Although transcriptions are frowned upon in some quarters, there can be no valid objection to them if they meet the need of the organist and if the music loses nothing in the arrangement. Some of the slower movements of Beethoven's piano sonatas, for instance, lend themselves admirably for use as voluntaries, as do sarabandes and airs from some of the classical suites. One can readily understand an objection to the transcription of orchestral music for, in most cases, the organ cannot do it justice.

Pieces with which people are apt to associate secular words are not recommended; although in these days when every classical theme is regarded as fair game by popular song writers, it is not always easy to avoid melodies which have become "popularized" in some objectionable way.

Vocal music which depends largely upon the words for its interest is seldom good in transcription. Airs from Handel's *The Messiah*—"He was despised" in Lent, and "I know that my Redeemer liveth" at Easter—are well enough known by everyone to add a seasonal note when played before or during a service; airs such as Bach's "Be Thou But Near" from the *Anna Magdalena Claires Book* are so beautiful in themselves that the absence of the words does not impair the listeners' enjoyment; but anthems or solos from obscure cantatas mean nothing to the congregation who do not know the words on which the music depends for interest and appropriateness.

The wise organist plays only music that he can play well, postponing excursions into difficult compositions until such time as he has acquired the necessary technical ability. There is a wealth of good music that is not difficult, and it is much more enjoyable to hear an organist play a simple piece well than to endure his struggles with something beyond his capabilities.

The Anglican service offers much scope for improvisation. Facility in improvisation and modulation should be acquired even at the expense of studying new pieces, for it adds tremendously to the service.

Very few organists explore fully the tonal possibilities of their instruments. There is an unhappy tendency to settle upon a few combinations of stops and to use them almost exclusively. It is wise to listen to groups of instruments, especially the full orchestra, whenever possible, studying the tonal effects, balance, etc., and to use the experience thus gained in altering one's combination pistons from time to time. Young organists are apt to use too much pedal. Perhaps the pride of achievement which accompanies a certain pedal dexterity leads them to show off their talents a little. The most important thing about pedalling is to know when to stop.

And, finally, the organist is advised to play rhythmically. His instrument is not one on which it is easy to stress initial beats in the measures, and he must use other devices—clean-cut phrasing, an occasional semi-staccato, a strict adherence to time—in order to give life to his playing. Organ music would be more highly regarded if all organists would strive to make their listeners feel the pulse of the music, instead of gliding lifelessly from chord to chord, vainly hoping that the expression pedal and changes of registration will compensate for the lack of rhythm.

§6 Education in Church Music

The organist and choirmaster who can spare some time for developing an appreciation of church music among the congregation would be well advised to do so.

Too many congregations stand mute during those parts of the service in which they should participate. Some choirmasters ask nothing more from their congregations than silence while the choir does the singing, but the fact remains that something is very wrong with a service in which the people do not feel free and ready to take their part. Unfortunately, our Prayer Books provide no pointing for the psalms, but there is no good reason for the people not joining in the hymns, canticles and responses.

Sometimes the congregation may be invited to remain for half an hour after the evening service for hymn practice. If the choristers mingle with the people to lend them encouragement, an immediate increase in volume may be noticed. Most people like to sing: the difficulty lies in overcoming their diffidence and getting them started. After a few familiar hymns are sung, some pointers on phrasing may be given and one or two tunes learned. Very few hymn tunes are too difficult to be learned quickly: anyone who is interested should have learned a tune after singing it or hearing it sung to three or four verses of a hymn. If two or three hymn practices go well, some attention may be given to the canticles and the responses. Eventually a few psalms may be learned, and opportunities may be given to the people to become more familiar with the music of the communion service, new chants, etc.

If congregational practices cannot be arranged, opportunities for group singing might be found at meetings of church societies.

The important thing is to convince the people that the music of the church is not some deep mystery of which the choirmaster is the high priest and the choir his privileged acolytes. Share the music with the people; take them into confidence, tell them what the music means and what the plans and ideals of the choirmaster are.

Much of the lack of interest on the part of the congregation is due to poor training in the Sunday Schools. The section of most hymnals devoted to "Hymns for Children" is of a definitely lower standard than the rest of the book. If the children's hymns do happen to be good, some Sunday Schools will disregard them in favor of a separate book which is sufficiently poor to meet the tastes of the Sunday School officials.

The threadbare excuse given is that children must sing "simple" hymns. One has no quarrel with simplicity if it is combined with excellence, but the musical perception of children is not nearly as low as their elders imagine it to be. After all, in choirs composed of men and boys only, the most involved music is sung by children from nine to fifteen years of age. It is far easier to teach good hymns and tunes to children than to their parents.

There is a real danger, too, that poor hymns may lower children's respect for the church. In communities where the appreciation of music is given prominence in the schools, the children will soon notice if the music in the church school falls below the standards set by secular teachers.

The number of Sunday Schools in which canticles are never chanted is amazing and discouraging. It is not surprising that in so many churches the service is sung by the choir alone.

These conditions often exist simply because there is no one in the Sunday School with sufficient musical knowledge and ability to improve the situation. One can scarcely blame a Sunday School superintendent or his teachers for not tackling a problem which they cannot handle; but it is a golden opportunity for the organist and choirmaster, and in most cases his assistance would be welcomed. The duties of a church musician lie in the future as well as in the present; and if he wants to be sure of a singing congregation and good material for his choir in years to come, he will find the Sunday School an excellent training ground.

While on the subject of education, it might be well to mention the part that the clergy play in the music of the church. The rector and his curate will be proficient in singing the versicles, of course, and their co-operation is essential when planning and preparing choral services. But they should also be asked to sing tenor or bass in hymns and other parts of the service which they sing with the choir. Nothing is more disconcerting to a small choir trying to sing harmony than a clergyman with a strong voice singing the melody. Anyone who sits in the chancel—clergyman or lay reader—should either assist the choir or remain silent, and the choirmaster has a legitimate complaint when someone else undertakes to "lead the singing" and nullify all the painstaking work that has been done at choir practice.

The duties of many clergymen do not permit regular attendance at choir practices (although some of the busiest of them manage to get there and render invaluable assistance to the choir) but if they enjoy singing they should certainly be encouraged to sing parts. They are intelligent men, and if they are musical enough to sing they should have little difficulty in learning to follow the notes. Most of them realize that this accomplishment is an asset to their work.

It is a pity that organists and choirmasters in most churches have to rely almost solely on their own efforts for the development of the practice and appreciation of church music in their own parishes. In some large cities, more or less assistance may be available from a university; in some localities summer courses in church music are held; but for church musicians in small communities there are no organized means for assistance.

Organists and choirmasters of several smaller churches might meet once a week or twice a month to hold discussions and solve their problems. It would be helpful to have the clergy attend these meetings, and choristers should be encouraged to attend. A definite programme, not only for each meeting but over an entire season, should be arranged if progress is to be made. Each parish in the district could, in turn, act as host and its choir be present either to illustrate certain points to be discussed or to serve as subjects for experiments.

While the discussion should be general, it might be well to have as "lecturer" one person who seems particularly qualified to speak on some phase of church music. The speaker might be an organist and choirmaster or a clergyman from the district or, if a specialist from outside the district is available, so much the better. In choosing speakers, care should be taken to invite only those who have an appreciation of the problems of a small parish. For instance, there would probably be no point in asking the cathedral organist to address a meeting in a rural district: doubtless he would be interesting, but he is too far removed from rural conditions to be helpful.

While a great deal of good work can be done by groups of organists and choirmasters acting on their own initiative, the weakness of such a course lies in its lack of official sanction.

It does seem reasonable to suggest that church music is the business and concern of the church itself. Certainly if music in many smaller parishes is not to deteriorate to the point where it is almost beyond saving, it must receive official impetus and encouragement.

Meetings such as those outlined above would become far more valuable if they were under diocesan auspices. The organists and choirmasters would gain enthusiasm from the knowledge that the church was endorsing their efforts, the clergy would be more likely to attend and contribute if they knew that the bishop was interested, and choirs (perhaps even congregations) would warm to a scheme that had the advantage of diocesan leadership.

A committee, working under the authority of the bishop, could draft a general course to be followed in each district or "clinic." Periodically, the organists and choirmasters, clergy, and any other interested people of three or four districts might meet at a central point to hear a choir which had been trained to illustrate points already covered by the course. The climax of the season's work could be a diocesan service at the cathedral.

Such a programme is well worth trying, and no one would be better pleased with the results than the bishop and clergy.

IV · THE SERVICES OF THE CHURCH

§1 General Notes

The services of the church as contained in the Book of Common Prayer are complete in themselves. By studying the italicized directions printed throughout the book (the *rubrics*) and referring to the tables of lessons, one could sit at home and read any of the services exactly as they are read in church. There is seldom any serious deviation from the Prayer Book forms. The differences which one may encounter in different parishes have to do not with the services themselves, but the manner in which they are conducted. Under certain conditions some omissions are made, but these need not trouble the organist or choirmaster if he has been warned of them by the rector.

In some churches additions are made, especially to the service of Holy Communion. These are usually parts borrowed from other liturgies, and may not be the same in all parishes. Most of such additions are made in very few churches, and one might never hear them used. On the other hand a few, such as the *Benedictus qui venit* and the *Agnus Dei*, although not authorized by the Prayer Book, are widely used and, in this manual, will be considered as accepted parts of the service.

While it is not necessary that anything precede, interrupt or follow the services proper, it is customary on Sundays and festivals to extend them by means of hymns, anthems, sermons, etc. The only guides for these parts of the services not covered by the Prayer Book are tradition and common sense. Happily, in spite of the lack of official direction, one may expect little variation from an accepted conventional form.

This manual attempts to cover all the slight variations of the service that are commonly encountered. Unusual occurrences and radical departures from what may be considered normal usage cannot be foreseen, but it is hoped that the organist and choirmaster of the average parish church will find herein sufficient information to enable him to perform his duties with confidence.

Although all services are treated as being fully choral, this fact should not be construed as an attempt to persuade organists and choirmasters to change the habits of congregations who prefer a said or partly said service. The remarks concerning music for parts of the service which are normally said in one's parish may be passed over, and the text resumed where it becomes applicable to one's needs. A said service is, after all, as proper as a choral one—is, indeed, preferable unless the choral parts are well done. It is not proper to mix the two: for instance, if the priest cannot or will not chant the versicles the choir should not chant the responses, and the *Amen* should not be sung at the end of a prayer that has not been intoned.

§2 Morning Prayer

The first service in the Prayer Book is the Order for Morning Prayer (often called *Matins* or *Mattins*). It is appointed to be read daily, although in some parishes the minister does not read it publicly in church every day.

When the choir is present, hymns and at least some parts of the service are sung. Even in churches where intoning is not favored, the canticles are generally chanted; while in cathedral practice the psalms, versicles and responses are also chanted and the prayers intoned. As has been said earlier in this book, many hold that no note for intonation should be given until after the first recitation of the Lord's Prayer, and that intonation should cease with the Third Collect. Such eminent church musicians as the editors of *The Cathedral Prayer Book*, however, provide for intoning from the beginning of and throughout the service, although limiting the use of inflections to that portion beginning after the first Lord's Prayer and ending with the Third Collect. Both usages are proper.

(i) It is customary for the organist to play a *prelude* or *voluntary* before the service begins. It is his privilege to assist in creating the proper atmosphere for the service, and his music should be chosen with some consideration for the season, the type of service, and the subject or theme which is to be dominant. Since the service proper begins on a note of penitence and confession, it would seem fitting that the voluntary be of a quiet nature calculated to induce a mood of reflection, although it need not be sombre or depressing. Meandering and unmelodious successions of chords seldom achieve the desired purpose: the theme should be definite enough to hold the attention of the congregation and prevent distraction.

Organists who invariably reach for the *vox humana* and *tremulant* with their left hands while turning on the motor with their right will probably not take the trouble to read a book like this, so there is no need to dwell upon the unhappy results of such a habit.

The congregation should understand that the voluntary is not designed to render whisperings and restless stirrings less noticeable, but that it is a part of the service worthy of the same attention and respect as any other part. But the congregation is not likely to take the voluntary seriously unless the organist himself recognizes and accepts the responsibility that is his. The clergyman, upon entering the church, should find the people if not inspired, at least in a receptive mood: he must be very disheartened when he finds them merely amused by some frivolous or sentimental air that the organist has been playing.

(ii) If a hymn is to be sung, it is well for the organist to time his voluntary so that he may bring it to a close by the time the hymn is to be played over. It is a good plan to arrange some sort of signal to be relayed to the organist a minute or two before the choir is ready to enter the church.

When the hymn is not sung in procession, the people stand as the choir enters and the voluntary continues until the choristers have taken their places. The minister will probably announce the hymn; but if he does not, the organist should begin to modulate in time to have the key of the hymn tune established by the time the tune is to be played over. Even if the hymn is announced it is as well to modulate either before or after the announcement, especially if the voluntary is in a key remote from that of the hymn tune.

If there is a processional hymn, the organist will try to end his voluntary as soon as the choristers have reached the place from whence the procession begins. Processional hymns are seldom announced (although they may be) and modulation to the key of the hymn tune should be effected by the time the tune is to be played over. The tune should be given out distinctly and not too loudly: the tempo should be exactly that in which the organist expects the entire hymn to be sung; and the choir should understand that no concessions will be made for dragging.

If part of the organ is located near the point at which the procession begins, the choir will be greatly assisted if that section of the organ is used for the first two or three verses of the hymn. If the entire organ is situated in the chancel, stops which speak distinctly (diapasons and flutes) will give the best support while the choir is still some distance from the organ. A tendency to drag can be corrected more easily by adding four-foot stops (or even the fifteenth) than by the use of reeds and mixtures.

The processional hymn is better sung in harmony. If the choir is so large that the aisle may be filled with men singing tenor and bass, and if it is feared that the congregation may be confused thereby, a descant may be used. The effect of the men singing the melody while still in the nave with the boys singing a descant while entering the choir is excellent.

If intoning is to commence immediately following the hymn, it is wise to choose a tune whose key-note is not the same as the note of intonation. One key too long sustained may become monotonous.

(iii) *The Sentences* or texts which are found on the first two or three pages of Morning Prayer mark the beginning of the service proper. Generally only one or two are used at a service. The Canadian and American Prayer Books provide certain sentences for special days, although the minister is not obliged to use them. The organist need not know beforehand how many or which sentences are to be read, since he has nothing in particular to do at their conclusion.

When there is no hymn, modulation will have to be made from the voluntary to key containing the note of intonation (unless the voluntary is in a key suitable for the purpose) and the note will be sounded when the choir and clergy are settled in their places. To avoid hurrying the minister or keeping him waiting, it is helpful to have a glance or nod from him when he is ready. A pre-arranged code of quiet glances and scarcely perceptible nods between the minister and the organist will prove a great help in keeping the service running smoothly.

When there is a hymn, the note of intonation is given as soon as it is finished. If any modulation is necessary, it should be made quickly. While a delay between the hymn and the sentences is not desirable, it is preferable to the harsh effect of the unprepared sounding of the G after an unrelated chord such as E major or A flat major.

It is assumed in this manual that the note of intonation is G, since that is usually the most convenient pitch for all concerned. However, another note may be given if it seems better suited. A tone or semitone will not make a great deal of difference to the choir and congregation, but it may mean much to a clergyman who finds it a strain to maintain G. The minister has to do most of the intoning, and his convenience should receive first consideration.

Incidentally, it is not necessary that this part of the service be intoned by the minister: often a layman is appointed for that purpose. In English cathedrals the intoning (and sometimes all the music) is entrusted to one of the canons who is known as the *cantor* or *precentor*. This arrangement is reflected in the directions given for antiphonal singing: parts marked *decani* are for that section of the choir on the dean's (or rector's) side of the chancel;

those marked *cantoris* are for the choristers on the same side as the cantor or canon precentor.

(iv) *The Exhortation* ("Dearly beloved brethren, the Scripture moveth us" etc.) follows the Sentences without pause. When intoned, it is not necessary for the organist to sound the note since the minister or cantor should be able to maintain the pitch after intoning the Sentences.

The Exhortation is frequently shortened, and the organist who has to sound a note for what follows should listen for the closing words: "unto the throne of the heavenly grace, saying after me." (In the American book the words "after me" do not appear.) The note for the Confession is sounded as the people kneel.

(v) *The General Confession* ("Almighty and most merciful Father; we have erred, and strayed from thy ways like lost sheep" etc.) is said by all present. The note of intonation may be the same as that which has been used for the Sentences and Exhortation, but it is often a minor third lower. Why humility and penitence can better be expressed on E than on G has never been explained, but many people think it seemly to drop to the lower note.

In order that the pitch may be maintained, it is generally desirable to supply an accompaniment when the congregation is monotoning. The organ should be played softly, providing just enough support to keep the people on pitch. Stops of the *celeste* type and the *tremolo* are not suitable for this purpose: if string quality is used, there should be enough flue stops drawn to insure definitude. It is in the accompaniment rather than by the note of intonation that the subdued atmosphere of humility may be strengthened. Minor chords may predominate, and the accompaniment may become a little brighter at the words: "according to thy promises." All this, however, is merely suggestive; the organist must be guided by his own taste.

Any chord which contains the note of intonation is suitable for the accompaniment, but the progressions should be logical. One would scarcely care to play a definite theme but, on the other hand, meaningless meandering is not good. Most service books contain accompaniments for the Confession, Lord's Prayer, Creed, etc. which will serve the organist in good stead until he can devise some of his own.

At the end of this and all prayers recited by the congregation, the *Amen* should be monotoned in normal fashion and in unison, not drawn out as in singing.

There is a setting of the Confession known as the *Ely Use* which provides inflections and harmonies. It could not, of course, form part of a service not fully intoned, and its use is more consistent in churches where psalms and responses are *sung* rather than *chanted* in normal speech rhythm. While the Ely Confession is not in general use, it is very beautiful; and it is used in many cathedrals and churches whose sanction can leave no doubt of its propriety.

To avoid a ragged beginning, many clergymen recite alone the first few words of the Confession (or any other part of the service said by the whole congregation), the people joining him at the end of the first phrase or repeating what he has already said. The organist should know his rector's policy in this matter.

At the end of the Confession, all remain kneeling except the minister who rises to pronounce the Absolution.

(vi) *The Absolution* ("Almighty God, the Father of our Lord Jesus Christ, who desireth not the death of a sinner" etc.) is said by the priest, or by the bishop if he is present. If the Confession has been intoned on G there will be no need to sound the note again; if the people have been monotoning on E, it may or may not be necessary to sound G for the Absolution. Most clergymen are so accustomed to the interval of a minor third that they will need no assistance from the organ; but if a minister is a little uncertain or will feel more confident at hearing the G, there is certainly no harm in sounding it.

After the Absolution (if intoned) the *Amen* is monotoned by all, either in unison or in harmony.

If the service is taken by a layman, as sometimes happens in cases of necessity, the Absolution cannot be used; and the organist should find out beforehand what prayer is to be said in its stead.

(vii) *The Lord's Prayer* is said by all kneeling. If it is intoned an accompaniment may be provided, although there is a strong feeling in the American church that the Lord's Prayer should be unaccompanied and, preferably, said in the natural voice. The organist may prefer to use fewer minor chords than in the Confession, and he may brighten his progressions and increase the tone a little at the words, "For thine is the kingdom."

It is not customary to use special settings of the Lord's Prayer at Morning and Evening Prayer, although they are frequently used in the service of Holy Communion.

(viii) *The Versicles and Responses* ("O Lord, open thou our lips" etc.). In churches where it is preferred that the early parts of the service be said in the natural voice, this will be the first occasion upon which the organist is called upon to sound a note for intonation—the first sounding of the organ since the opening hymn was ended.

The first versicle and response are generally pitched a fifth lower than the others (on C) but it is quite proper to take G if the cantor finds that note more convenient. The note is sounded as soon as the Lord's Prayer is ended.

If the earlier parts of the service have been intoned, it should not be necessary to give the cantor the note, but it may be sounded if he so desires.

The versicles and responses should be chanted simply, with a complete absence of dramatic effect. The comparative merits of Ferial and Festal Responses have been discussed in an earlier chapter.

It will be noted that immediately before the versicle, "Glory be to the Father" etc., the people stand.

In parishes where a plain service is preferred, the versicles and responses may be said in the natural speaking voice.

(ix) *The Invitatories* or *Invitatory Antiphons* appear only in the American book, but they have long been used in a few English and Canadian churches and are becoming more widely adopted.

Apart from the collect and the lessons, and perhaps one of the opening sentences, the Order of Morning Prayer is the same for all seasons of the church year. The Invitatories, coming at a point in the service which marks the transition from penitence to praise, add a welcome seasonal note.

For the benefit of English and Canadian organists and choir-masters who are not familiar with the Invitatories, they are reprinted here.

On the Sundays in Advent: *Our King and Saviour draweth nigh; O come, let us adore him.*

On Christmas Day and until the Epiphany: *Alleluia! Unto us a child is born; O come, let us adore him. Alleluia!*

On the Epiphany and seven days after, and on the Feast of the Transfiguration: *The Lord hath manifested forth his glory; O come, let us adore him.*

On Monday in Easter Week and until Ascension Day: *Alleluia! The Lord is risen indeed; O come, let us adore him. Alleluia!* (Some hold that this Invitatory should be sung from the Monday following the First Sunday after Easter; but, since the American Book of Common Prayer is the only one in which the Invitatories are officially sanctioned, it seems reasonable to regard its directions as authoritative.)

On Ascension Day and until Whit Sunday: *Alleluia! Christ the Lord ascendeth into heaven; O come, let us adore him. Alleluia!*

On Whit Sunday and six days after: *Alleluia! The spirit of the Lord filleth the world; O come, let us adore him. Alleluia!*

On Trinity Sunday: *Father, Son, and Holy Ghost, One God; O come, let us adore him.* (Another version: *One God in Trinity, and Trinity in Unity; O come, let us adore him.*)

On the Purification and the Annunciation of the Blessed Virgin Mary: *The Word was made flesh, and dwelt among us; O come, let us adore him.*

On other festivals for which proper Epistles and Gospels are appointed: *The Lord is glorious in his saints; O come, let us adore him.* (In most churches, restricted to Saints' Days.)

The Invitatories are sung (rarely said) immediately before the Venite, of which they are intended to form an integral part. Occasionally they are repeated after the Venite. At the close of the last preceding response ("The Lord's Name be praised") the organist should quickly effect any necessary modulation and, with the choir and people, proceed without pause to the Invitatory, and then to the Venite which should be in the same or a closely related key.

(x) *Venite, exultemus Domino* (in the English and Canadian books, Psalm 95; in the American book, Psalm 95, verses 1 to 7, and Psalm 96, verses 9 and 13) follows the Responses or the Invitatory without interruption. If there is no Invitatory, modulation should be made after the last response and the chant played over before the Venite is chanted: if the Invitatory is used, little or no modulation will be necessary, and it is preferable to proceed to the Venite without waiting to play over the chant.

When the Responses are said in the natural voice, the chant is given out as soon as the words, "The Lord's Name be praised," have been uttered. It is most unusual for the Venite to be *said* when the organist and choir are on duty.

It is customary to provide single chants for the Venite but, as there are few interesting single chants, and as even the interesting ones tend to become monotonous when too often repeated, many choirmasters prefer to use double chants. When a double chant is used for a canticle or psalm of uneven verses, the second half of the chant must be repeated for one verse—usually the fifth verse of the Venite.

The *Gloria Patri* ("Glory be to the Father, and to the Son, and to the Holy Ghost; as it was in the beginning, is now, and ever shall be, world without end. Amen") is chanted at the close of the Venite, all psalms and most canticles. In some churches, the choir faces the altar while the Gloria Patri is chanted.

There are some exceptions to the use of the Venite. The English book directs that it is not to be chanted in its usual place on the nineteenth day of the month, but with the psalms for the day. A strict observance of this rubric would make it impossible to sing an Invitatory on the nineteenth of the month, for the Invitatory can only precede the Venite in its usual place.

The Canadian book, on the other hand, provides for the chanting of the Venite in its regular place on the nineteenth day, and its omission from the psalms appointed for the day.

The American book offers no rule, but the Venite is usually chanted before the psalms as in the Canadian church. A direction is given that Psalm 95 (the Venite as contained in the English and Canadian books) may be used instead of the version in the American book (parts of Psalms 95 and 96).

For certain festivals, substitutes for the Venite are provided: in the English book, for Easter Day; in the Canadian book, for Christmas Day, Good Friday, Easter Day, Ascension Day and Whit Sunday; in the American book, for Easter Day and Thanksgiving Day. These "anthems," as they are called, are found in the Prayer Books before the collects of the days for which they are appointed. (The American book provides for the omission of the Venite on Ash Wednesday and Good Friday.)

If no Invitatory is appointed for a day on which an "anthem" replaces the Venite, the organist proceeds to give out the chant for the "anthem" as soon as the response, "The Lord's Name be praised," is finished.

The Venite or "anthem" ended, the organist awaits the announcement of the psalms.

(xi) *The Psalms* are, in the Prayer Books, divided into sixty sections—one section for each morning and evening in the month. (The psalms for the thirtieth day are repeated on the thirty-first.)

The English book contains a table of *Proper Psalms on Certain Days;* a similar but considerably extended table appears in the Canadian book immediately preceding the Psalter.

The American book, in the table of *Psalms and Lessons for the Christian Year,* appoints suitable psalms for every morning and evening in the church year, although the divisions according to the days of the month may be used if preferred.

The organist plays over the chant as soon as the psalms are announced. There is no need for modulation from the key in which the Venite was chanted: the break for the announcement should be sufficient.

The chant should be played over even when the psalms are to be said, for the Gloria Patri is chanted after each psalm and after each division of Psalm 119 whether the psalms are said or chanted.

Chants should be chosen to suit the psalms for which they are used. As was remarked in an earlier chapter, any Anglican chant will "fit" any psalm; but obviously, "O praise the Lord of heaven; praise him in the height" will require a brighter chant than will "Save me, O God; for the waters are come in, even unto my soul."

Double chants for longer psalms, and a change of chants during very long psalms will help to avoid monotony. The last half of a double chant will have to be chanted an extra time when used for a psalm with an odd number of verses. All psalters indicate at which verses the repetition should be made.

When two or more psalms are used, the chants are generally in closely related keys; but there is no reason why a psalm should not be chanted in a key remote from that which preceded it, providing the organist makes his modulation effective and brief.

When the choir has four parts on each side of the chancel, it is well to chant the psalms antiphonally, the *decani* (south side) taking the first verse, the *cantoris* (north side) the second, and so on. The Gloria Patri and any verses marked *full* are chanted by the entire choir. "Full" verses are, as a rule, of a joyful nature and may be made occasions for descants or unison chanting with a somewhat elaborate accompaniment.

The accompaniment for the psalms is generally restrained. "Clear" stops, medium-voiced diapasons and flutes predominating, lend the best support. Pedals are sparingly used, and sixteen-foot manual tone is undesirable. Avoid color and sound effects. Even some organists who should know better have been guilty of imitating the twitter of birds and the roar of thunder when such noises have been mentioned in the psalms.

If unison chants are used—and they are strongly recommended for choirs without four dependable parts—the accompaniment may be varied, and should not be subdued to the point where the harmonies are not in evidence.

The psalms ended, the choir and congregation sit down: and the clergyman or reader, who has proceeded to the lectern during the last chanting of the Gloria Patri, will read the lesson.

(xii) *The First Lesson*, from the Old Testament or, occasionally, from the Apocrypha, is introduced by the words "Here beginneth the —th verse of the —th chapter of the book of X." The organist should be prepared to proceed to the canticle that follows when the reader says: "Here endeth the First Lesson."

(xiii) *Canticles following the First Lesson.* The English and Canadian books offer a choice of two canticles to be used after the First Lesson; the American book has three.

Te Deum laudamus is one of the church's great hymns of praise. It is divided into three sections, and generally two or three chants in related keys are used. It is to be noted that the Gloria Patri is not chanted at the close of the Te Deum.

There are many eleborate settings of the Te Deum which may be used at Morning Prayer or, on occasions of thanksgiving, at any other service.

The version in the American book differs slightly from that in the English and Canadian books. An English or Canadian choirmaster using an American edition, or an American using an English edition should make sure that the necessary changes in the words can be made without doing violence to the music.

Benedicite, omnia opera (*Domini*) is traditionally used in Advent and Lent and, in many churches, during the period from Septuagesima to Lent also.

The Benedicite is so lengthy that at least one change of chant is desirable. Many shortened settings are available, the words, "Praise him and magnify him forever," not being chanted for every verse, but after groups of abbreviated verses.

The Gloria Patri follows the Benedicite in the English and Canadian churches, but not in the American church which has an added verse to replace the Gloria. The version in the English and Canadian books contains one verse which does not appear in the American book.

Benedictus es, Domine is provided in the American book only as an alternative canticle after the First Lesson. It is followed by the Gloria Patri.

(xiv) *The Second Lesson* is read from the New Testament, and the words, "Here endeth the Second Lesson," are the organist's cue to give out the chant for the canticle that is to follow.

Occasionally only one lesson is read, in which case it is from the New Testament, and will be closed with the words, "Here endeth *the* Lesson." The canticle will be one of those appointed for use after the Second Lesson.

Banns of Marriage are published immediately after the Second Lesson. The rector will warn the organist when banns or any other announcements are to be read at this point, so that the playing over of the chant for the canticle may be delayed.

In some churches the baptismal service is occasionally held after the Second Lesson.

(xv) *Canticles following the Second Lesson.* Of the two canticles which may be used, the Benedictus is generally preferred, especially from Advent to Whit Sunday when the various phases of Christ's life on earth are unfolded more or less chronologically. The American church permits a shortened form (four verses only) except in Advent. The Gloria Patri follows the canticle.

The Benedictus should not be used as a canticle when it is read as part of a lesson or the gospel. When Prayer Book lectionaries are used, it forms part of the lessons on the following days:

In the English church, on March 25 (the Feast of the Annunciation) at Morning Prayer; on September 24 at Evening Prayer;

In the Canadian church, on the Wednesday following Trinity Sunday, and the Wednesday following the Seventeenth Sunday after Trinity at Evening Prayer; on the Eleventh Sunday after Trinity at Morning Prayer;

In the American church, on the Third Sunday in Advent, the day before Christmas, and the Friday following Trinity Sunday at Morning Prayer.

In all Prayer Books the Benedictus forms part of the gospel for St. John Baptist's Day (June 24).

Jubilate Deo (Psalm 100) may be chanted after the Second Lesson except when it occurs among the psalms appointed for the day. Being a short psalm, a bright single chant is appropriate, and the Gloria Patri follows.

The Benedictus is generally preferred to the Jubilate because it is a New Testament canticle and can be chanted only in this place, whereas the Jubilate is used at least once a month as part of the psalter.

"Service settings" of these two canticles are plentiful.

(xvi) *The Creed* (generally the *Apostles' Creed*) is said by all present, standing. As soon as the canticle after the Second Lesson is finished, the organist sounds the note for the intonation, G being the most convenient pitch, although in a few churches the Creed is intoned a minor third lower. The minister may say a few words alone and then be joined by the people, or the whole congregation may begin at once. Local customs vary.

An unobtrusive accompaniment may be provided for the Creed. Most organists prefer a change to the minor key at the passage beginning "Suffered under Pontius Pilate" (modulation to C minor is natural and easy) and fuller, brighter chords at "The third day he rose again from the dead."

The choir should be trained not to hurry the Creed, the Lord's Prayer and other parts of the service which are intoned by all the people. True, the responsibility for setting the pace rests with the cantor, but he can be overpowered and carried away by a choir that will not listen to him. It is a good plan to intone these parts of the service at choir practice with the cantor present.

In the American book, the *Nicene Creed* (that generally associated with the service of Holy Communion) is given as an alternative to the Apostles' Creed.

In the English and Canadian books, the *Creed of St. Athanasius* is sometimes used in place of the Apostles' Creed. It is not included in the Order for Morning Prayer, but appears separately in the Prayer Books after the service of Evening Prayer. (In the English book, the heading is *At Morning Prayer*, and in many service books it appears under the heading *Quicumque vult.*)

The English book directs that the Creed of St. Athanasius be used on Christmas Day, the Epiphany, Easter Day, Ascension Day, Whit Sunday, Trinity Sunday, and the Feasts of St. Matthias, St. John Baptist, St. James, St. Bartholomew, St. Matthew, St. Simon and St. Jude, and St. Andrew; but in most parishes it is used only on Trinity Sunday. The Canadian book merely says that it *may* be used on any day of the year. The American book omits it altogether.

Musical settings are based on ancient usage and, while some slight variations may be found, they may be grouped into two general classes: those which require an inflection in the first part of the verse (or statement) only, and those which have both parts of the verse inflected. The choirmaster will be able to make a choice from any reliable service book.

After the chanting of the Benedictus or the Jubilate Deo, the organist gives out the notes for the first half of the verse (G-A-G) which is generally intoned by the cantor alone. The creed from this point may be intoned responsively (cantor and people), antiphonally, the boys (or women) and the men taking the verses in turn, or the whole creed may be intoned by all present.

Intoning in unison is much to be preferred, since the oft-repeated short harmonic phrase would tend to become monotonous. Variety is provided by the organist who may improvise as freely as the voice part allows. For organists unskilled in improvisation (and the Creed of St. Athanasius is not easy to accompany well) accompaniments such as those in *The Cathedral Prayer Book* and *The Oxford Psalter* will be invaluable.

It will be noted that the Creed of St. Athanasius ends with the Gloria Patri, similarly inflected.

While the Creed could be recited on one note, it is seldom so intoned. It is, of course, proper to say any of the creeds in the natural voice.

(xvii) *Responses following the Creed.* ("The Lord be with you," etc.) When the Creed has been intoned, it is not necessary to sound the note for the Versicles and Responses that follow, for the pitch will already be established.

Some settings give a single, unaccompanied note for the response, "And with thy spirit"; most provide harmonies.

At the words, "Let us pray," all kneel.

(xviii) *Responses and Lord's Prayer.* (This section does not apply in the American church, as it is not contained in the American Prayer Book. It is noted in a rubric, however, that the Lord's Prayer may be said if it has not been said earlier in the service.)

The words, "Lord, have mercy upon us; Christ, have mercy upon us; Lord, have mercy upon us"; are intoned as soon as the people are on their knees. The first petition is intoned by the priest only; the second and, often, the third by all the people, either in unison or in harmony. When a settting of the Responses gives no harmonies for this part of the service it is better unaccompanied, although a quiet accompaniment is in order if it is necessary for maintaining the pitch.

The Lord's Prayer follows, ending, be it noted, with the words, "But deliver us from evil. Amen." When the Lord's Prayer is monotoned, an accompaniment may be provided. In some churches it is monotoned a minor third lower than the rest of the service. It is recommended that, with the possible exception of the General Confession, the whole service be intoned in one key. Frequent changes in the note of intonation are not desirable or traditional.

(xix) *Versicles and Responses* ("O Lord, shew thy mercy upon us," etc.) follow the Lord's Prayer in the English and Canadian books, and the words, "Let us pray," in the American book. These responses may be accompanied or not at the discretion of the choirmaster.

(xx) *The Collects* are, generally, three in number; that appointed for the day, one for Peace, and one for Grace. The last is referred to as the Third Collect even when an extra seasonal collect is used after that for the day (for instance, in Advent or Lent).

If the rest of the service has been intoned, the Collects will probably be intoned also. The Amens may be in unison or harmony, accompanied or not. Generally all Amens except the last consist of the subdominant and tonic chords (Plagal Cadence); the one after the Third Collect being the dominant and tonic (Perfect Cadence). But *The Cathedral Prayer Book* prescribes the dominant-tonic progression after all three collects.

After the Third Collect, the organist may improvise until the people have risen from their knees.

(xxi) *The Anthem* (*or Hymn*). The traditional place for the anthem is after the Third Collect. If no announcement is made, the organist's improvisation is used as an opportunity to modulate to the key in which the anthem is to be sung, and may continue until the people are settled in their pews and the choristers are ready.

Some clergymen prefer to announce the words of the anthem, not as a reflection on the choir's diction, but because it is consistent with the custom of giving the sources of those parts of the service not contained in the Prayer Book (the lessons, the text for the sermon, etc.). The most natural and dignified form of announcement is something like the following:

The words of the anthem are those of the Collect for Sexagesima Sunday: "O Lord God, who seest that we put not our trust" etc.

or

The words of the anthem are those of hymn number three: "New every morning is the love our waking and uprising prove."

or

The words of the anthem are from the sixtieth chapter of the Book of Isaiah: "Arise, shine, for thy light is come; and the glory of the Lord is risen upon thee."

An announcement such as "The choir will now sing an anthem!" is quite unnecessary and undignified. The choirmaster cannot very well tell his rector what should be said, but diplomatic suggestions are in order when, as rarely happens, one is working with a clergyman who has a weakness for saying and doing things in an awkward manner.

When the congregation is provided with a printed service list, the words of the anthem should certainly appear thereon; and when there is no such list, it is well for the minister to read the words. The anthem, like any other part of the service, is for the edification of the congregation, and it is a definite waste of effort when the people do not know the words that are being sung.

When there is no anthem, a hymn is generally sung instead. In some churches, a hymn is sung in any case, the anthem being postponed until later in the service.

Sometimes, in order to shorten the service, neither anthem nor hymn is sung, the prayers that follow being read immediately after the Third Collect.

(xxii) *Prayers* which follow the Collects in the Order of Morning Prayer are said in the natural voice if the early parts of the service (Sentences, Exhortation, Confession, Absolution and Lord's Prayer) have been said. If intonation was begun at the beginning of the service, however, it is proper to intone these prayers also. Half a dozen chords of modulation after the anthem or hymn will give the people time to kneel, and serve as preparation for the note of intonation.

If the clergyman reads in his natural voice, the organist need not be greatly concerned about any prayers that may be substituted for or added to those prescribed: but if the prayers are to be intoned, he should know of such substitutions or additions in advance in order to be ready for the Amens.

If the *General Thanksgiving* ("Almighty God, Father of all mercies," etc.) is recited by all the people and intoned, an accompaniment is advisable.

These prayers ended, the organist may improvise softly until the people have risen from their knees and the clergyman is standing at the prayer desk ready to announce the hymn. This is often considered a convenient time for making other announcements concerning future services, church meetings, etc.

(xxiii) *A Hymn* is sung, towards the end of which the minister who is to preach will take his place in the pulpit.

(xxiv) *The Sermon* will not, of course, require any activity on the part of the organist. Most clergymen end their sermons with the ascription: "And now, to God the Father, God the Son, and God the Holy Ghost, be ascribed, as is most justly due, all might, honor, dominion and power, now and forever," after which the people say, "Amen." In some churches this Amen is sung, which is improper unless the clergyman intones the ascription.

After the ascription, the minister proceeds to the place from where he will repeat the Offertory Sentence—generally the sanctuary step. If the pause is longer than a moment or two, the organist may fill the gap by improvising a few chords softly.

(xxv) *The Offertory Sentence* is a text reminding the people of their duty to be liberal and charitable. When there is no sermon, the Offertory Sentence follows the closing prayers of Morning Prayer (xxii).

Immediately after, or immediately before the Offertory Sentence, the clergyman announces the hymn or anthem.

(xxvi) *The Offertory*. During the offertory a hymn is generally sung, although in some churches an anthem (or even a second anthem) is used instead. As an alternative, the organist may play a solo.

When the sidesmen wait at the rear of the church until the hymn is finished (they will certainly wait for the end of an anthem) the organist should continue to play while they bring the offering to the chancel, during the presentation of the alms, and until the sidesmen have returned to their places in the nave.

Very often, during the presentation of the alms, an appropriate verse is sung, such as "All things come of Thee, O Lord," etc. or "We give Thee but Thine own," etc. When this is done, the organist will time his modulation to arrive at the desired key at the moment the minister turns towards the altar with the offering, and will improvise in that key until the sidesmen have left the chancel.

(xxvii) *Prayers and Benediction.* One or two prayers and the Benediction follow the Offertory. These may be intoned or not, at the pleasure of the rector.

Sometimes a more or less extensive setting of the Amen, such as Stainer's Fourfold or Sevenfold, is used after the Benediction, even when the priest has been speaking in his natural voice.

In many churches the Benediction ends the service, and the organist plays quietly while the clergy and choir retire. Often, however, a hymn closes the service, in which case the organist improvises while the priest kneels after the Benediction and until he rises in readiness for the hymn.

(xxviii) *The Closing Hymn* is announced in some churches, unannounced in others. When not announced, the organist's improvisation should take the form of a modulation to the key in which the hymn is to be sung.

When the hymn is a *recessional*, the point at which the choristers begin to leave their stalls should have been determined beforehand in order that the last of the procession may reach the exit as the Amen is sung.

Most of what has been said about the processional hymn applies to the recessional. If there is an objection that singing in harmony leaves tenors and basses in the church after the sopranos have proceeded beyond earshot, four or five good sopranos and altos may remain inside the door until the Amen is sung.

The congregation kneels for a few moments after the hymn, and quiet improvisation is in order during that short period.

In a few churches—very few, fortunately—the clergyman recites a dismissal prayer before leaving the church. This is definitely out of line with tradition and good practice: any such prayer should be said before the Benediction. It is customary to have a dismissal prayer for the choir after they have reached the choir room; and it is, no doubt, a misconception regarding the purpose of this prayer which has resulted in a few clergymen saying it in the church.

While the people are leaving the church, the organist generally plays a *postlude*. It need not always be loud and stirring music: somewhat graver music may fittingly close some services.

Shortened Morning Prayer. Occasionally the words, "Let us humbly confess our sins to Almighty God," are substituted for the Exhortation; or all that part of the service from the Opening Sentences up to and including the first recitation of the Lord's Prayer is omitted. These abbreviations are not usually made at a choral service, however.

Sometimes the First Lesson and the canticle following it are omitted. If the organist and choirmaster can follow the entire service with confidence, he is not likely to be troubled by omissions providing he is warned of them beforehand.

§3 Evening Prayer

The Order for Evening Prayer (often called *Evensong*) is appointed to be read daily. It is similar to Morning Prayer in so many respects that it will be necessary to consider here only those points in which it differs.

The parts of the service have been allotted the same numerals as the corresponding parts of Morning Prayer, and those marked with an asterisk are subject to the same directions and comment.

(i) *Organ Prelude.**

(ii) *Hymn.**

(iii) *The Sentences.**

(iv) *The Exhortation.**

(v) *The General Confession.**

(vi) *The Absolution.** (The American book provides an alternative form of absolution.)

(vii) *The Lord's Prayer.**

(viii) *The Versicles and Responses.** When this part of the service is intoned, the organist will cease playing after the last response and await the announcement of the psalms, since the Invitatories (ix) and the Venite (x) are not used at Evening Prayer.

(xi) *The Psalms.** The American book provides that at the end of the psalms for the day, instead of the Gloria Patri *may* be said or sung the *Gloria in Excelsis* ("Glory be to God on high, and on earth peace, good will towards men," etc.).

(xii) *The First Lesson.**

(xiii) *Canticles following the First Lesson.* The canticles are not the same as those at Morning Prayer. The English and Canadian books prescribe the *Magnificat* or the *Cantate Domino* (Psalm 98); the American book directs that either one of these or the *Bonum est confiteri* (Psalm 92) be used. Each is followed by the Gloria Patri.

Since the psalms are read or chanted as part of the selection of psalms for the days of the month, the Magnificat is the generally preferred canticle unless it is read elsewhere in the service.

In the Prayer Book lectionaries, the words of the Magnificat are appointed to be read as part of the second lesson on the following days:

In the English church, on March 25 (the Feast of the Annunciation of the Blessed Virgin Mary) at Morning Prayer; on September 23 at Evening Prayer;

In the Canadian church, on the Tuesday following Trinity Sunday, and on the Tuesday following the Seventeenth Sunday after Trinity at Evening Prayer; on the Tenth Sunday after Trinity at Morning Prayer;

In the American church, on the Second Sunday in Advent, on the Thursday following the Fourth Sunday in Advent (unless Christmas intervenes), and on the Wednesday following Trinity Sunday at Morning Prayer.

(xiv) *The Second Lesson.**

(xv) *Canticles following the Second Lesson* are the *Nunc Dimittis* or the *Deus misereatur* (Psalm 67) or, in the American church only, *Benedic, anima mea* (Psalm 103), after any of which the Gloria Patri is chanted.

The Nunc Dimittis is generally preferred unless the words are included in a lesson or the gospel for the day. It is part of the lessons appointed by the Prayer Book lectionaries for the following days:

In the English church, on March 27 at Morning Prayer; and on September 26 at Evening Prayer;

In the Canadian church, on the First Sunday after Christmas at

Morning Prayer; on the Friday following Trinity Sunday, and on the Friday following the Seventeenth Sunday after Trinity at Evening Prayer;

In the American church, on the Second Sunday after Christmas, and on the Monday following the First Sunday after Trinity at Morning Prayer.

In all Prayer Books the words of the Nunc Dimittis are included in the Gospel for the Feast of the Purification of the Blessed Virgin Mary (February 2).

(xvi) *The Creed.** (The Creed of St. Athanasius is not used at Evening Prayer.)

(xvii) *Responses following the Creed.**

(xviii) *Responses and Lord's Prayer.** (Not included in the American Book.)

(xix) *Versicles and Responses.** (But note, that in the American book there are six versicles and responses instead of only two as at Morning Prayer.)

(xx) *The Collects.** (The Second and Third Collects are not the same as at Morning Prayer.)

(xxi) *The Anthem* or *Hymn.**

(xxii) *Prayers.**

(xxiii) *Hymn.**

(xxiv) *The Sermon.**

(xxv) *The Offertory Sentence.**

(xxvi) *The Offertory.**

(xxvii) *Prayers and Benediction.** A short evening hymn is sometimes used as a vesper before or after the Benediction.

(xxviii) *Closing Hymn.**

§4 The Litany

The directions concerning the Litany vary slightly in the Prayer Books.

The English book directs that it be used on Sundays, Wednesdays and Fridays, and at such other times as the minister may deem advisable.

The Canadian book provides for its use after the Third Collect at Morning or Evening Prayer, or before the Communion Service, or as a separate service on Sundays, Wednesdays, Fridays, the Rogation Days, and at other times considered appropriate by the minister. The rubric requires that it be used at least once a month on Sunday.

The American book prescribes the Litany after the Third Collect at Morning or Evening Prayer, or before the Communion Service, or as a separate service, but does not specify the days on which it is to be used.

In actual practice, the Litany is used on Wednesdays and Fridays, perhaps oftener in penitential seasons, and occasionally on Sundays. In any case, its use will be governed by the discretion of the rector, and the choirmaster need only act upon instructions.

When the choir is not present (and sometimes when the choir is present) the Litany is said, and the organist and choirmaster will have no duties in connection with it.

Generally the Litany is intoned in churches where the responses at Morning and Evening Prayer are intoned. The most widely used is the *Ferial* setting, which permits the words to be uttered naturally with the same quantity and stress as in ordinary speech. It may be in unison or in harmony, accompanied or unaccompanied. It is best chanted in harmony, and caution requires a soft accompaniment. If there is no accompaniment, the responsibility for maintaining the pitch rests almost entirely upon the cantor; and it is expecting a great deal to ask him to go through the Litany unaided without deviating at least a little from the pitch on which he began.

Another setting, known as *Tallis's Litany*, must, because of a hint of floridness in its harmonies, be *sung* and requires, therefore, a less natural utterance of the words. It is an excellent setting for use in churches where measured time is employed in the canticles and psalms.

If the Litany follows the Third Collect at Morning or Evening Prayer, the anthem (or a hymn) generally intervenes. When the anthem is finished, the organist may improvise quietly while the clergyman makes his way to the litany desk (generally situated at the foot of the choir steps), making sure to arrive at the desired key by the time the people are ready to kneel. The first note, or the first two notes of the intonation may then be sounded.

If the Litany is to be used before the Communion Service, or as a separate service, it may be preceded by a hymn. Improvisation and any necessary modulation are in order while the minister proceeds to the litany desk (which, by the way, is often known as the faldstool).

When preparing the Litany, the choir should take care to observe punctuation marks. The meaning of a petition may be altered or lost by the failure to observe a comma.

The choirmaster will have no difficulty in following the Litany from his service book, and will make sure that the rules of good chanting are applied.

In some churches the last two prayers (and in some Canadian churches, the General Thanksgiving) are said in the natural voice because they were not included in the older Prayer Books. (They are not included in the present day American book.) If this is not considered sufficient reason for saying them, they may be and generally are properly intoned.

Following the Litany, Morning or Evening Prayer proceeds as usual: Hymn, Sermon, Offertory, etc.

When used as a separate service, the Litany may be followed by a hymn which, if there is no sermon, may serve as the offertory hymn. From this point the service will proceed as at Morning or Evening Prayer.

When the Litany is used before the Communion Service, it may be followed by a hymn; or the priest may proceed to the Communion Service at once, in which case the Litany will probably end just before the Lord's Prayer.

Whatever follows the Litany, the organist may improvise while the minister proceeds from the litany desk to the place from which he will continue the service.

§5 The Communion Service

The Communion Service (officially called *The Order for the Administration of the Lord's Supper or Holy Communion*, and sometimes referred to as the *Eucharist* or the *Mass*) is the chief service of the church.

At a choral service, there are sometimes introduced fragments of earlier masses and liturgies, unauthorized by the Prayer Books but so generally used that they are considered parts of the service proper by many church people. These additions sanctioned by long usage will be considered as we go through the service, but will be plainly indicated as "not prescribed in the Prayer Book."

When selecting music for the Communion Service, the choirmaster will find many complete settings available. The better ones (and they include some of the easier ones) are written to form a complete whole rather than a group of unrelated musical fragments. The themes of the Creed, for instance, will perhaps be repeated or recalled in the Gloria in Excelsis; the Sanctus *motif* may reappear in the Benedictus qui venit, etc. Miscellaneous settings of parts of the service, chosen from chant books or the back of hymn books, may serve admirably, but they do lack unity.

What may be considered a complete setting for the Communion Service includes the Kyrie, Gloria Tibi, Credo, Sursum Corda, Sanctus, Benedictus qui venit, Agnus Dei, Pater Noster, Gloria in Excelsis and Amen. Many settings leave out one or more of these parts and, while the omissions may be quite proper according to the usage the composer has in mind, it is disappointing when the missing part happens to be one which the choirmaster uses at his service. In such a case, a substitution will have to be made from another setting; or the incomplete setting may be discarded in favor of one which includes the required part.

As a rule, the choral parts of the service mentioned above are *sung* (not chanted) although more are sung in some churches than in others. It is not uncommon to hear at least some of the prayers intoned, and in many churches other parts of the service, such as the Epistle, the Gospel, the Comfortable Words and the Prefaces are intoned and inflected as well. In order that this manual may be of the greatest possible assistance to the organist and choirmaster, we shall assume a service for which music is supplied at every opportunity. It must be understood, however, that anything that can be sung or intoned may also be said in the natural speaking voice; and that we are not trying to persuade the choirmaster to have intoned any parts of the service which his rector and congregation prefer to have said.

(i) An *Organ Prelude* or *Voluntary* will probably open a choral service. The organist should be particularly careful in his choice of music for this most important of all services. Good churchmen spend some time in preparation for their communion, and await the service in a spirit of devotion which should not be disturbed by light or frivolous music. The organist should bring out his best, striving to preserve and deepen the atmosphere of devotion and reverence. The voluntary continues until the choir and clergy have entered the church and are ready to proceed with the service; or, when there is a processional hymn, until the choristers have taken their places at the point at which the procession is to begin.

(ii) *A Hymn* appropriate to the season usually precedes the Communion Service proper. If the hymn is not announced, it is well to modulate briefly from the key in which the voluntary was played.

Remarks concerning the processional hymn in the section on Morning Prayer apply here if the first hymn is sung in procession.

(iii) *The Introit* (not prescribed in the Prayer Book) is a short, quiet anthem which may be sung (preferably kneeling) while the priest is making final preparations at the altar. The words should be such as will assist the people in their preparation for communion, rather than seasonal. Anthems beginning with words such as, "Jesu, Word of God Incarnate," "O Saviour of the world," "Lord, for Thy tender mercies' sake," or "Come unto Me," are suitable.

As soon as the first hymn is finished, the organist should improvise briefly, making any necessary modulation to the key of the Introit.

An Introit may be used even when there is no hymn, the organist modulating from the voluntary and arriving at the desired key as the choir and people kneel. In this case, a quiet hymn may be substituted for an anthem for use as an Introit.

On Easter Day and other festivals on which an "anthem" is substituted for the Venite at Morning Prayer, (Christmas Day, Good Friday, Ascension Day and Whit Sunday in the Canadian church; Thanksgiving Day in the American church), the seasonal "anthem" may be used in the place of the Introit providing Morning Prayer and the Communion Service are not combined. Because of the nature of the words, it should be sung or chanted by the people standing. The seasonal "anthem" is hardly an introit in the usual sense of the word, and most people would prefer to use it later in the service, perhaps as the Gradual.

(iv) *The Lord's Prayer*, which begins the service proper, is said by the priest alone. It is not usually intoned, although it may be if the priest prefers. Intoned or said, the choir and people refrain from joining in the Amen.

When the Lord's Prayer is said in the natural voice, the organist simply stops playing after the hymn or Introit; when the priest has requested a note, brief modulation should be made to the desired key.

(v) *The Collect* (beginning "Almighty God, unto whom all hearts be (are) open,") may be intoned. If the Lord's Prayer has been intoned, it will not be necessary for the organist to repeat the note; if the Lord's Prayer has been said in the natural voice, the note of intonation should be given as soon as the priest says, "Amen."

The Amen after the Collect should be sung by all if the prayer has been intoned; said otherwise.

In deciding upon the note of intonation, the choirmaster should have in mind the key in which the musical setting of the Communion Service is to be sung. G is a good note for a setting in C, G or E flat major; F serves well for F and B flat major and D minor; F sharp for B minor, etc.

(vi) *The Ten Commandments* (or *Decalogue*) may be properly intoned by the priest, but are often said in the natural voice even when the prayers are intoned. The American book provides a shortened form which may be used if desired.

The *Kyrie Eleison* is sung after each commandment. The words of the Kyrie are the same after the first nine commandments, but a variation occurs after the tenth.

The music of the Kyrie may be the same after all commandments (excepting the allowance made for the change of wording after the tenth commandment) or it may vary with each repetition. Some composers make use of the descant and faux bourdon.

The Kyrie should not be dragged. There is no irreverence in singing parts of the Communion Service at a fairly brisk tempo. The organ accompaniment should be moderately soft, and some change of tone quality introduced for each repetition of the Kyrie.

(vi*a*) *The Summary of the Law* ("Hear what our Lord Jesus Christ saith: Thou shalt love the Lord thy God with all thy heart," etc.) is prescribed in the Canadian and American books as an alternative for the Ten Commandments. The Canadian book stipulates that the Ten Commandments must be read at least once on Sunday and on great festivals at the chief service of the day (some clergymen are careless regarding this rubric); the American book requires that the Ten Commandments be read at least one Sunday in each month.

The Summary of the Law is read immediately after the Collect (v). In the Canadian church, the Kyrie usually sung after the tenth commandment is used, substituting the words, "and write *both* these thy laws," for "and write *all* these thy laws."

In the American book, the Summary of the Law is followed by the *Three-Fold Kyrie:* "Lord, have mercy upon us; Christ, have mercy upon us; Lord, have mercy upon us"; which may be said or intoned if the particular setting being used does not contain music for it.

The American Prayer Book permits the reading of the Summary of the Law after and in addition to the Ten Commandments. The Three-Fold Kyrie may follow, although the Prayer Book does not so direct.

The organist and choir should be informed beforehand when the Summary of the Law is to be substituted for the Ten Commandments in order that they may be prepared.

(vii) *Prayer.* In the English and Canadian churches there follows one of the two prayers for the Queen ("Almighty God, whose kingdom is everlasting, and power infinite," etc. or "Almighty and everlasting God, we are taught by thy holy Word," etc.); in the American church, the prayer beginning, "O Almighty Lord, and everlasting God," etc.

If the prayer is intoned, the organist should make sure that the priest is given his note after the last repetition of the Kyrie. All join in the Amen.

In the American church, there follows: "The Lord be with you; And with thy spirit; Let us pray," which is said or intoned depending upon whether the preceding prayer has been said or intoned.

(viii) *The Collect of the Day* follows. When two festivals fall upon the same day, it is customary to read only the collect of the festival which takes precedence, although the collect for the secondary festival may be read later (perhaps after the Offertory or before the Benediction). There is no hard and fast rule, however, and the priest may prefer to read both collects at this point. From the Second Sunday in Advent until Christmas, and from the First Sunday in Lent until Easter, two collects must be read as directed by the rubrics. (See Chapter II, §2 and §6.)

The Collects, Epistles and Gospels are found immediately before the Communion Service in the English and Canadian books, immediately after in the American book.

If the Collect is intoned, the priest will take his note from the prayer preceding. All join in the Amen, rise from their knees, and are seated.

(ix) *The Epistle* is generally read by the priest in his natural voice, although it is sometimes intoned with proper inflections. A priest who can properly intone the Epistle will not need a note from the organ, but will take his note from the Collect.

At the words, "Here endeth the Epistle," the people stand.

(x) *The Gradual* (prescribed in the American book only, but used in many English and Canadian churches) is generally a hymn chosen not only for its seasonal words, but for the agreement of its subject with that of the Epistle or the Gospel, or both.

In early liturgies the Gradual was a psalm, and the use of a psalm is still proper. It is also proper, although unusual, to sing an anthem at this point, care being taken that the words have a bearing upon the theme of the Epistle or the Gospel.

On days when an "anthem" is substituted for the Venite at Morning Prayer, and when there has been no other opportunity for singing the seasonal "anthem," it may be introduced very effectively as a Gradual. A point in favor of using it here is the fact that the words of the "anthem" are printed with the Collect, Epistle and Gospel for the day, and there is no necessity for the people to turn to another part of the Prayer Book at short notice.

If the hymn, psalm or anthem is announced the organist will, of course, consider the announcement his cue to proceed; if there is no announcement, the tune, chant, or introduction to the anthem should be played over as soon as the priest says, "Here endeth the Epistle."

(xi) *The Gospel* is announced immediately after the Gradual or, if there is no Gradual, after the Epistle.

The Canadian and American books direct that the *Gloria Tibi* ("Glory be to thee, O Lord") be said or sung immediately after the announcement of the Gospel; and, while no such direction is contained in the English book, the Gloria Tibi is sung more often than not in the English church also.

Most settings for the Communion Service include music for the Gloria Tibi; many, especially later English settings, do not. If the composer has not provided music, a substitute setting may be used, or the Gloria Tibi may properly be said or monotoned. (But, of course, if the priest intones the Epistle and Gospel it is scarcely consistent to say the Gloria Tibi in the natural voice.)

The organist should be prepared to play the Gloria Tibi immediately after the priest says: "The Holy Gospel is written in the —th chapter of ——, beginning at the —th verse."

While the wise organist follows the entire service in his Prayer Book, it is particularly important that he read the Gospel, for the priest does not announce its close. As soon as the priest has read the concluding words, the organist plays the *Gratias Tibi* ("Thanks be to thee, O Lord") in the English and Canadian churches, or the *Laus Tibi* ("Praise be to thee, O Christ") in the American church.

The Gratias Tibi or Laus Tibi is a musical sentence the same as or complementary to the Gloria Tibi. If the Gloria Tibi is said or monotoned, the Gratias Tibi will be repeated in like manner.

Immediately after the Gratias Tibi or, in English churches where the Gratias Tibi is not used, immediately after the Gospel, the organist sounds the note for the Nicene Creed.

(xii) *The Creed* (or *Credo*) used in the Communion Service is the Nicene Creed; although the American book permits the use of the Apostles' Creed instead except on Christmas Day, Easter Day, Ascension Day, Whit Sunday and Trinity Sunday.

Most settings of the service contain music for the Nicene Creed: some elaborate and assuming the proportions of an anthem, others relatively simple. In some parishes it is objected that the singing of the Creed prevents the congregation from participating, and, however disappointed the choirmaster may feel at being asked to forego the singing of a beautiful setting, he cannot deny the validity of the objection.

When the Creed is not sung at a choral service, it is generally monotoned on a note taken from the final chord of the Gratias Tibi or Laus Tibi. An organ accompaniment is provided to maintain the pitch, becoming quieter in the section that speaks of the Incarnation, perhaps modulating to a related minor key when the Passion is recalled, and brightening noticeably at the part that tells of the Resurrection.

(xiii) *Announcements* and *Banns of Marriage* usually follow the Creed, the people being seated.

(xiv) *A Hymn* or *Anthem* generally follows the announcements. A hymn will be announced, and the clergyman who is to preach will take his place in the pulpit before it is finished. An anthem may or may not be announced, and at its conclusion the organist may play softly while the minister proceeds to the pulpit.

(xv) *The Sermon* is then preached, and at its conclusion the people stand while the minister repeats the ascription. The Amen which follows the ascription should be said in the natural voice unless the minister intones the ascription (which is unusual).

To avoid an awkward pause while the minister is returning to the sanctuary, the organist may improvise softly, ceasing when the minister turns to say the Offertory Sentence.

(xvi) *The Offertory Sentence* is here said, although if there is no sermon the sentence may follow the announcements or the Creed.

If a hymn is to be sung during the Offertory, it will be announced immediately after or immediately before the Offertory Sentence.

(xvii) *The Offertory*. A hymn is usually sung while the offering is received, although an anthem may be sung instead, or the organist may play a solo.

The organist should continue to play softly while the sidesmen are bringing the offering to the chancel, during the presentation of the alms, and until the sidesmen have resumed their places in the nave.

If something is sung during the presentation of the alms, the organist should time his modulation to the required key to coincide with the turning of the priest towards the altar.

(xviii) *The Prayer for the Church Militant*. The sidesmen having resumed their places after the presentation of the alms, the priest will say: "Let us pray for the whole state of Christ's church (militant here on earth)" at which the people kneel.

The prayer which follows (beginning, "Almighty and everliving God, who by thy holy Apostle hast taught us," etc.) is intoned if other prayers have been intoned, although it may be said in the natural voice. All join in the Amen.

(xix) *The Exhortations*. In the English and Canadian books, there follow three Exhortations, only the third of which is sometimes used at the Communion Service.

The first (beginning, "Dearly beloved, on —day next I purpose, through God's assistance, to administer" etc.) is read at some service preceding that of Holy Communion, and is actually a formal announcement read in the natural voice.

The second (beginning, "Dearly beloved brethren, on — I intend, by God's grace, to celebrate the Lord's Supper," etc.) is also an announcement to be read at an earlier service when the people are negligent in coming to Communion. It is also said in the natural voice.

The third (beginning, "Dearly beloved in the Lord, ye that (who) mind to come to the holy Communion," etc.) belongs to the Communion Service proper, and may be intoned if the prayers are intoned. Some clergymen prefer to say it in the natural voice even when earlier parts of the service have been intoned. The English book directs that the Exhortation *shall* be read; the Canadian book, that it *may* be used.

In the American book, these Exhortations are conveniently printed at the end of the Communion Service; but that which forms part of the service proper ("Dearly beloved in the Lord, ye who mind to come to the holy Communion," etc.) is placed first. The use of this Exhortation is left to the discretion of the priest except on the First Sunday in Advent, the First Sunday in Lent, and Trinity Sunday when, according to the rubric, it *shall* be said.

(xx) *The Invitation* ("Ye that (who) do truly and earnestly repent you of your sins," etc.) may be intoned or said by the priest immediately after the Prayer for the Church Militant or after the Exhortation. If intoned, no note need be given, for the priest will continue on the same pitch as before the Invitation.

In some churches the Exhortation, Invitation, Confession, and Absolution are said in the natural voice even when all the rest of the service is intoned.

(xxi) *The Confession* ("Almighty God, Father of our Lord Jesus Christ, Maker of all things," etc.) when intoned, is sometimes taken on a lower note (usually a minor third below the principal note of intonation) but this is by no means a general rule. The note should be sounded by the organist, who will play a soft accompaniment to maintain the pitch.

A traditional and beautiful setting of the Confession with inflections and harmonies is available. Its occasional use is not recommended, since it will tend to confuse the congregation: used regularly, the people will quickly become accustomed to it. It is better not to use inflections for the Confession unless the Comfortable Words are also to be inflected.

The Confession is often said in the natural voice.

(xxii) *The Absolution* ("Almighty God, our heavenly Father, who of his great mercy" etc.) is pronounced by the priest, or by the bishop if he is present.

If the Confession has been intoned on a lower note, the priest may or may not require assistance from the organ in returning to the principal note of intonation. (The organist should be informed beforehand when the priest wants his note sounded.) If the Confession and the Absolution are on the same note, the priest will need no help.

The Absolution may also be said in the natural voice.

(xxiii) *The Comfortable Words* (being the four short scriptural passages prefaced by the words: "Hear what comfortable words our Saviour Christ saith unto all that (who) truly turn to him:"). If the Confession and Absolution have been intoned, the Comfortable Words will also be intoned; if the Confession has been inflected, the Comfortable Words will be inflected. It does not follow, however, that the Comfortable Words will be said in the natural voice because that which precedes them has been said. It is customary in some churches to resume intoning at the Comfortable Words after the Invitation, Confession, and Absolution have been said. When such is the case, the organist should sound the note of intonation after the Absolution.

If the Comfortable Words are inflected, the priest may proceed alone, or a soft accompaniment such as that found in *The Cathedral Prayer Book* may be used.

Of course, the Comfortable Words may be, and often are, said in the natural voice.

(xxiv) *The Sursum Corda* (being the versicles and responses beginning, "Lift up your hearts") is included in many musical settings of the Communion Service. Any intoning that is done after the

Offertory should be on a note that leads gracefully to the Sursum Corda.

If the priest has intoned the Comfortable Words, he will proceed unassisted to the opening words of the Sursum Corda; if he has been speaking in his natural voice, he will require a note.

When the traditional inflections are used for the Comfortable Words, the traditional Sursum Corda should also be used whether another version is included in the musical setting or not. Composers who omit music for the Sursum Corda do so because they expect the traditional inflected form to be used. If it is omitted from the musical setting and the Comfortable Words are not inflected, the Sursum Corda may be monotoned, or music may be borrowed from another setting.

(xxv) *The Preface* ("It is very meet, right, and our bounden duty," etc.) may be monotoned by the priest on a note taken from the final chord of the Sursum Corda, or may be inflected if the Comfortable Words have been inflected. The inflected Preface may be accompanied or not, depending upon the wishes of the priest. Unless the organist is unusually proficient in improvisation, he will do well to use an accompaniment from the service book; if he prefers to use his own, he should at least have worked it out beforehand and, if possible, rehearsed it with the priest.

If the organist accompanies the Preface, he must remember that on Trinity Sunday the words, "Holy Father," are omitted, and one of the Proper Prefaces mentioned below is used.

Except upon certain festivals, the priest will read both paragraphs of the general Preface without interruption, the organist holding himself in readiness to play the Sanctus after the words: "Therefore with Angels and Archangels, and with all the company of heaven, we laud and magnify thy glorious Name; evermore praising thee, and saying."

(xxvi) *Proper Prefaces* are inserted between the two paragraphs of the general Preface on certain festivals and for seven days after: in all churches, on Christmas Day, Easter Day, Ascension Day, Whit Sunday and Trinity Sunday; in the Canadian church, on the Feast of the Epiphany as well; in the American church, on the Feasts of the Epiphany, the Purification, the Annunciation, the Transfiguration and All Saints.

The Proper Prefaces are said, intoned or inflected in the same manner as the general Preface, of which they form a part. The organist's signal for the Sanctus is invariably the same: "Therefore with Angels . . . evermore praising thee, and saying."

(xxvii) *The Sanctus* ("Holy, holy, holy, Lord God of hosts," etc.) is sung immediately after the words, "evermore praising thee, and saying."

All settings for the Communion Service include music for the Sanctus, and it is generally sung even in churches where the service is not intoned.

Although the Comfortable Words, Sursum Corda and Preface may have been traditionally inflected, it is quite proper and usual to use more modern settings for the Sanctus.

(xxviii) *Benedictus qui venit* (not prescribed in the Prayer Books): "Blessed is he that cometh in the Name of the Lord. Hosanna in the highest."

In many churches, the Benedictus qui venit is sung immediately after the Sanctus. If the music for both parts is contained in the one setting, the transition will be easy and natural: if, however, music for the Benedictus qui venit has to be borrowed from another setting, care must be taken to select one whose key and general style are consistent with those of the Sanctus.

In many other churches, it is preferred to postpone the singing of the Benedictus qui venit until after the next prayer. It can be omitted entirely, of course, since it is not contained in the Prayer Books.

It becomes necessary here to consider the English and Canadian books and the American book separately; for, while what follows is substantially the same in all Prayer Books, the order is not the same.

(xxix Eng. & Can.) *The Prayer of Humble Access* ("We do not presume to come to this thy Table, O merciful Lord," etc.) follows in the English and Canadian books. It may be said in the natural voice, or intoned. All join in the Amen.

(xxx Eng. & Can.) *Agnus Dei* (not prescribed in the Prayer Books): "O Lamb of God, that takest away the sins of the world, have mercy upon us," (sung twice); "O Lamb of God, that takest away the sins of the world, grant us thy peace."

Music for the Agnus Dei is included in most settings of the Communion Service. When a substitution is made, or when miscellaneous settings are used, care must be taken that the Sanctus, Benedictus qui venit and Agnus Dei are in the same key, or in keys so closely related that the same note of intonation may precede all three.

In many churches, the Benedictus qui venit is sung here instead of after the Sanctus, and the singing of the Agnus Dei is deferred until after the prayer that follows. Whichever is used, Benedictus qui venit or Agnus Dei, the organist should begin it immediately after the Amen which ends the Prayer of Humble Access.

(xxxi Eng. & Can.) *The Prayer of Consecration* ("Almighty God, our heavenly Father, who of thy tender mercy," etc.) is one of the most solemn parts of the service. It may be said or intoned, and all join in the Amen.

In the American church, after the Sanctus and, perhaps, the Benedictus qui venit, there follow:

(xxix Amer.) *The Prayer of Consecration, the Oblation, the Invocation and the Lord's Prayer* without pause. These may be said in the natural voice or intoned. Even if the Consecration, Oblation and Invocation are said, the Lord's Prayer (*Pater Noster*) may be intoned, or sung to music contained in the setting of the Communion Service. If the Lord's Prayer only is intoned or sung, the organist must be ready to play as soon as the priest has said: "And now, as our Saviour Christ hath taught us, we are bold to say."

The Benedictus qui venit may be sung after the Lord's Prayer if it has not already been sung. In view of the fact that this part of the service ends with all the people saying, singing or intoning the Lord's Prayer, it would seem preferable in the American church to sing the Benedictus qui venit immediately after the Sanctus.

(xxx Amer.) *The Prayer of Humble Access* ("We do not presume to come to this thy Table, O merciful Lord," etc.) may be said or intoned, all joining in the Amen.

(xxxi Amer.) *The Agnus Dei*, although not prescribed in the Prayer Book, may be sung here instead of the *Hymn* which the rubric permits. Whether the Agnus Dei or a hymn is used, it should be sung immediately after the Prayer of Humble Access, the choir and congregation kneeling.

From this point, the order of the service is much the same in all three Prayer Books.

(xxxii) *The Communion* is administered to the clergy, then to the choir, then to the congregation; and during this time music is provided. The organist will probably find it convenient to take communion at other than a choral service; first, because his absence from the organ bench will make necessary a period of silence at a time when it is not desirable; second, because his duties occupy all his attention and leave no opportunity to compose his mind and his thoughts in preparation for communion.

The music at the Communion should be the best of which the organist is capable. It should be soft enough not to distract the people from their devotions; if there are no soft stops on the organ, it might be better not to play at all. Of course, no self-respecting organist will be guilty of playing sentimental hymn tunes with the *vox celeste, vox humana* and *tremulant* being used to the exclusion of all else.

Since the organist may have to play for some time, he is advised not to rely upon improvisation unless he is very good at it. There are many quiet compositions well suited to this use.

In many churches, a hymn is sung during the Communion, or, if there are many communicants, perhaps two hymns may be used. Instead of singing the hymn right through, it is a good plan to sing two or three verses, then to improvise for two or three minutes before resuming the hymn. The choir will have to be alert for the organist's signal to resume the singing of the hymn.

The singing of Communion hymns is an excellent test of the choir's ability to sing softly, but it must be emphasized that soft singing does not necessarily mean slow singing. While the tempo of the Communion hymn will be somewhat leisurely, it must not be so slow as to make good phrasing difficult or impossible.

It is well to allow the choir to sing part of the hymn unaccompanied when it is capable of doing so.

The choirmaster who is trying to introduce plainsong tunes finds an excellent opportunity for doing so during the Communion. The tunes blend well with the nature of the service, they will not confuse the people who will not be trying to sing them during this part of the service, and the ears of the congregation will have the chance to become accustomed to them.

The singing of hymns may rob the organist of an opportunity to play complete pieces, but there is no reason why he cannot use as interludes short passages of pieces in the same key as the hymn tune.

It may be necessary to open the swell box a little to cover the slight commotion caused by the people approaching and leaving the altar rail.

Sometimes the supply of consecrated bread and wine is exhausted before all have received Communion, and it is necessary for the priest to pause and consecrate more. The organist must be prepared for such a contingency. If the priest is seen to approach the credence table (on the south side of the altar) for further supplies, the organist should be ready to stop playing, or to interrupt a hymn at the end of the verse that is being sung. When the priest has made the necessary preparations and stands facing the altar, the music should cease. Since the organist cannot see plainly when the priest is ready, some signal not perceptible to others may be arranged—the priest may adjust his stole or make some other slight movement that will pass unnoticed by the people. The entire Prayer of Consecration is not repeated. The priest will begin at the words, "Who, in the same night that he was betrayed, took Bread," (in the American church, "For in the night in which he was betrayed," etc.) or "Likewise after supper he took the Cup." In either case, when the words, "in remembrance of me," are said, the organist will play the Amen (or the people will say it) and the service will continue as if there had been no interruption.

When the priest has ministered to the last of the communicants, he kneels before the altar for a few moments. The organ is further reduced and, if the prayer that follows is to be intoned, any necessary modulation is made to the desired key. The note of intonation is sounded as the priest rises to his feet.

(xxxiii) *The Lord's Prayer* (in the English and Canadian books only) may be said, intoned or sung. Some settings of the service include music for the Lord's Prayer.

In the American church, the prayer that follows, preceded by the words, "Let us pray," is said or intoned immediately after the Communion, the Lord's Prayer having been repeated earlier.

(xxxiv) *The Thanksgiving* is then intoned or said, all joining in the Amen. The English and Canadian books permit the use of either of two Thanksgivings: "O Lord and heavenly Father, we thy humble servants," etc., or "Almighty and everliving God, we most heartily thank thee," etc. The American book contains only the second form.

(xxxv) *The Gloria in Excelsis* ("Glory be to God on high, and in (on) earth peace, goodwill towards men," etc.) is then sung.

As soon as the Amen at the close of the preceding prayer has been said or sung, the organist plays the first few notes of the Gloria in Excelsis while the people rise. Most settings contain a more or less elaborate Gloria in Excelsis, but some provide a fairly simple chant.

At the conclusion of the Gloria in Excelsis, the people kneel again, and the priest may insert one or two prayers which he considers desirable.

(xxxvi) *The Benediction,* intoned or said, closes the service proper. The Amen that follows is often an elaborate one.

After the Benediction there is a lull while the priest consumes any consecrated bread and wine that may remain, and cleanses the communion vessels. During this time, a short hymn or anthem may be sung kneeling, but the more general practice is for the organist to play softly.

The priest kneels before the altar when he has finished; and as he rises, the organist plays the chant or tune that follows.

(xxxvii) *The Nunc Dimittis* or a *Hymn* closes the service in most churches. If Morning Prayer has been combined with Holy Communion and the words of the Nunc Dimittis have been read as part of a lesson, it should not be used here; neither can the Nunc Dimittis be used on the Feast of the Purification when it will have been read as part of the Gospel.

A closing hymn should be seasonal in character, or one that speaks of renewed strength and resolution.

The choir may leave the church during the singing of the Nunc Dimittis or hymn, or after. The people will kneel for a few moments during which the organist will play softly, and the postlude will follow.

§6 Publick Baptism of Infants or Holy Baptism

Baptism is generally a separate service at which the organist and choir are not present. On the rare occasions when music is required, it will consist only of hymns before and after the service, and a prelude and postlude if the organist considers them desirable.

There are times, however, when Holy Baptism is combined with the service of Morning Prayer. The organist will be informed beforehand at what point Morning Prayer will be interrupted for baptisms: traditionally it is after the Second Lesson, although some clergymen prefer to have baptisms after the anthem or hymn which follows the Third Collect.

If baptism follows the Second Lesson, the priest will make his way to the font (generally situated at the west entrance to the church) as soon as he has said, "Here endeth the Second Lesson." In some churches where there is sufficient space at the west end to accommodate them, the choristers precede the priest and take positions near the font. To avoid a silent interval, it is well that the organist play softly until the priest is ready to proceed with the baptismal service.

If baptism follows a hymn, the priest will probably go to the font during the singing of the last stanza or two.

The service of Baptism is generally said; but if Morning Prayer is intoned, it is quite proper and not at all unusual to give the priest a note for part of the baptismal service. The general practice is for the priest to read in his natural voice those parts of the service which are addressed to the parents and godparents, and to intone the prayers.

The question, "Hath this Child been already baptized or no?" and the Exhortation beginning: "Dearly beloved, forasmuch as," etc. are said.

The prayers which follow (two in the English and Canadian books, one in the American book) may be intoned.

The passages of Scripture, and the further Exhortation which follows, are said.

The prayer beginning, "Almighty and everlasting God, heavenly Father," etc. may be intoned.

The questions to the godparents, and their replies, are said.

The four short prayers, the first beginning, "O merciful God, Grant that the old Adam in this child," etc. (in the American book: "O merciful God, grant that like as Christ died and rose again," etc.) may be intoned, as may the versicles and responses which follow in the American book and the longer prayer which precedes the act of baptism in all books.

The child is then baptized, and intonation may be resumed at the Lord's Prayer and continued through the prayer or prayers following.

In the English and Canadian books, a Charge to the godparents follows.

When the service of Baptism has followed the Second Lesson, Morning Prayer will be resumed at the canticle generally chanted after the Second Lesson. There is no need to wait for the choir and clergy to return to the chancel before beginning the canticle: they can sing as they are returning.

If Baptism has followed the anthem or hymn after the Third Collect, the service cannot be resumed until the priest has returned to the chancel, and the organ may be played softly while he is making his way thither.

It is likely that Morning Prayer will not be read beyond the Third Collect.

§7 The Order of Confirmation

At Confirmation, baptized persons renew and accept responsibility for the promises and vows made on their behalf at baptism, and may afterwards be admitted to the Holy Communion.

Since the time of the Confirmation depends chiefly on the convenience of the bishop, it may be at a morning or evening service, on Sunday or during the week. It may be a separate service, although it is generally combined with Morning or Evening Prayer, or with Holy Communion.

If Confirmation is to be a separate service, it will probably be preceded by a hymn. If the hymn is to be sung in procession, it should be a fairly long one; for it is customary for the confirmation candidates to enter the church after the choir, and they should have reached their pews before the hymn is ended.

The bishop takes his place at the top of the choir steps; and if he has not assumed that position by the time the hymn is ended, the organ may be played softly until he does.

The service proper is generally followed by a hymn, sermon, offertory, etc., as at Morning and Evening Prayer.

If Confirmation is combined with Morning or Evening Prayer it often (but by no means invariably) follows the anthem or hymn after the Third Collect.

When there is to be a celebration of the Holy Communion, Confirmation may precede the Communion Service, or it may come after the Gospel and Gratias Tibi (or Laus Tibi) and be followed by the Creed.

The organist and choirmaster should seek instruction from his rector concerning every detail, for these occasional services are most likely to present awkward moments. Although, broadly, the same in very church, there are many opportunities for slight variations in procedure. They cannot be too carefully planned to avoid gaps of silence.

Although the Order of Confirmation is often read in the natural voice, there is no reason for not intoning part of it. Indeed, in churches where Morning and Evening Prayer are intoned, it is only consistent that the Confirmation, a festival service, should be intoned also.

The first part of the service, in which the candidates are presented, addressed and questioned, is said in the natural voice.

The versicles and responses beginning, "Our help is in the Name of the Lord," etc. may be intoned, as well as the prayer that follows. Many chant books do not contain music for the responses at occasional services, but settings are available.

Then follows the actual Confirmation, when the candidates kneel before the bishop for the Laying on of Hands. There is no music during this period.

When all the candidates have been confirmed and have returned to their places, a note may be sounded and the remainder of the service (from the words, "The Lord be with you") may be intoned. A hymn is then sung, and Morning or Evening Prayer or the Communion Service continues from the point at which it was interrupted. If Confirmation has been after the Gospel at the Communion Service, the Creed may follow at once instead of a hymn.

§8 The Solemnization of Matrimony

A marriage service is one of the most difficult to keep within the bounds of propriety. There are at many weddings guests who are not church people, and who are not aware that reverence is expected in the Anglican church on all occasions. Sometimes even the principals seem to forget that the wedding service is not a secular festival. There is very little that the organist and choirmaster can do to regulate the behavior of the congregation—that difficult duty belongs to the rector—but he can and should resist suggestions for music that is not suitable for the church.

If there is a rehearsal, the organist and choirmaster can at least set an example of good behavior. When the rector and organist are jocular at the rehearsal—and some of them are—one should not be surprised if there is some levity at the wedding.

The organist generally goes on duty fifteen or twenty minutes before the hour appointed for the wedding. He remembers that any music unsuitable for a church service is unsuitable for a church wedding. His mission is to inspire—to create an atmosphere of reverence, not to amuse and entertain the waiting congregation with a *vox humana–tremolo* version of "My heart at thy sweet voice."

If the service is to be choral, the entry of the choir may be effected by a processional hymn, or the choir may proceed in silence from the main entrance of the church.

If a processional hymn is used, the choir may be followed immediately by the bridal party; or the bridal procession may begin when the hymn is ended and the choristers are in their places, the organist playing a wedding march.

If there is no opening hymn, the choir may enter before the bridal party during the playing of the wedding march; or the wedding march may be deferred until the choristers have reached their stalls. The choir should not attempt to keep step with the wedding march, whatever the bride and her attendants may choose to do. And in no case should the choir assemble in the church before the service is ready to begin.

If the choir is not present, the organist plays the wedding march for the bridal procession. Someone should accept the responsibility of notifying the organist (and the choir, if present) when the bride is entering the church.

If the organ has soft stops, the organist may play throughout the service. The music should always be subordinate, and should not prevent the voices of the priest and the bride and groom from being heard by the congregation.

The first part of the service is always said in the natural voice, but after the groom has repeated the words beginning, "With this ring I thee wed," etc., a note may be given for the prayer that follows (in the American church, for the several prayers) and all join in the Amen.

The priest then says in his natural voice, "Those whom God hath joined together let no man put asunder. Forasmuch as *N*. and *N*. have consented together in holy wedlock," etc.

A note may be given for the Blessing ("God the Father, God the Son, God the Holy Ghost, bless, preserve and keep you"; etc.).

In the American church, the service ends with the Blessing; but in the English and Canadian churches, the Amen should be followed immediately by one of the appointed psalms. During the chanting of the psalm, the priest proceeds to the altar, and the bride and groom to the sanctuary step.

As soon as the Gloria Patri after the psalm has been chanted, the organist may sound the note of intonation if the versicles and responses and the prayers which follow are to be intoned.

After the prayer beginning, "Almighty God, who at the beginning did create our first parents," etc., there may be an Exhortation—either that contained in the Prayer Book or some other. There should be no music during the Exhortation, but at its close (or after the prayers, if there be no Exhortation) the organist plays softly while the bride and groom and their attendants repair to the vestry to sign the register.

If the organist alone is on duty, he plays while the register is being signed: if a soloist or the choir is present, a solo, anthem or hymn may be sung. Good wedding anthems are not plentiful, but there are some. Solos heard at church weddings are often in shocking taste. Some of the favorites—"O Promise Me," "I Love You Truly," "Because," etc.—whatever their merits in other surroundings, are totally unsuitable for a church service. If the organist does not oppose their use, the rector should.

The solo, anthem or hymn ended, the organist plays quietly until the bridal party is ready to emerge from the vestry, when he modulates to the wedding march. Better still, if the choir is present, a recessional hymn may be sung.

Strictly speaking, the choir should precede the bridal party down the aisle. Certainly they should not follow it, or remain in the church after the bridal party leaves. If some bride feels that the choir in procession will detract from her wedding march, the choir may retire before she leaves the vestry.

If there is a communion at a wedding, the Communion Service follows its usual form. In the Canadian book, a proper collect, epistle and gospel are provided at the end of the marriage service; in the American book, in the section devoted to collects, epistles and gospels.

§9 The Burial of the Dead

At a funeral service, the choir may be present, or the organist may be on duty alone. When there is a choir, the service may be largely choral, or singing may be confined to the hymns and, possibly, the psalm.

If the choir is not present, the singing even of hymns is difficult, for many of the congregation are not in the mood to sing. It would be better to omit hymns altogether, although one does not care to oppose the wishes of the bereaved family if they ask for hymns.

We shall assume that the service is to be choral, remembering that any part of it may be said in the natural voice if local custom demands.

It is advisable for the organist to take his place a few minutes before the service, having first arranged for someone to keep watch and warn the choir when the funeral cortege reaches the church.

The music before the service should be quiet and serious. Sentimentality should be avoided.

As the funeral cortege approaches, the choir should assemble at the church door (inside or outside) and slowly precede the body up the main aisle. During the procession, the Sentences beginning, "I am the resurrection and the life," etc., are said by the priest or sung by the choir. (The music for the Sentences is generally an adaptation of the traditional setting of Merbecke.)

When the organist sees the choir (or the minister, if the choir is not present) start towards the chancel, he will play very softly in order that the Sentences may be heard, or modulate in preparation for the singing of the Sentences. If the procession is a long one and the distance between the west door and the chancel is great, a short interlude may be played between sentences. When such breaks occur, the choir should have been coached very carefully, for they are not likely to be in a position to take a starting signal from the organist.

If the choir and clergy reach their places before all the mourners are in their pews, the organist will continue to play softly until the congregation is settled.

One of the appointed psalms is then said or chanted, with or without accompaniment. The Gloria Patri follows, of course.

Sometimes, but not often, a hymn is sung after the psalm.

Then is read the Lesson, followed by a hymn or anthem.

The Apostles' Creed is sometimes said or intoned at this point.

Part of the service is omitted at the church (to be said at the grave later) and what follows varies as the priest deems fitting. The organist need not be at a loss, however, for the balance of the service is said or monotoned. There are no responses. It is well to provide a soft accompaniment for the Creed and the Lord's Prayer as usual, in order that the pitch may be maintained.

After the last prayer, the organist improvises until the clergy and choir rise from their knees. The choristers immediately move towards the main entrance, preceding the body to the door. The Nunc Dimittis or a hymn is sometimes sung while the choir is proceeding to the west door.

The organist continues to play until all have left the church.

If the burial is to take place in the churchyard (as is still sometimes the case) the choir may precede the body to the graveside.

The service at the grave generally opens with the Sentences beginning, "Man that is born of a woman hath but a short time to live," etc.

Music is provided for this part of the service but, since it must of necessity be sung unaccompanied, it should not be attempted except by a well-trained choir, and some means of giving them the required pitch should be devised.

If there is a communion at a funeral, the collect, epistle and gospel will be found in the Canadian book at the end of the burial service; in the American book, in the section set apart for collects, epistles and gospels.

§10 Commination Service or Penitential Office

A Commination or, as it is called in the American book, a Penitential Office, is appointed to be read on Ash Wednesday, and is rarely used on other occasions.

The service generally follows the Litany, although it is sometimes used after the Third Collect at Morning or Evening Prayer (without the Litany), and sometimes as a separate service.

In the English and Canadian churches, after the Litany, or the Third Collect at Morning or Evening Prayer, or a hymn, the priest reads the first part of the Commination Service from the prayer desk or, less frequently, from the pulpit. The section beginning, "Brethren, in the primitive Church there was a godly discipline," etc., is addressed to the people and said in the natural voice.

At the words, "which ye affirm with your own mouths the curse of God to be due" (or, in the Canadian church, "which ye affirm with your own mouths the wrath of God to be revealed"), a note may be given for what follows.

The recital of the sins which incur the wrath of God may be intoned. It is customary to use a low note (a minor third below the usual note of intonation) and there should be no accompaniment. The Amens should not be prolonged, but monotoned quickly in unison. These sentences are often said, even when later parts of the service are to be intoned or chanted.

The Exhortation which follows is said in the natural voice, and as the priest says, "Amen," the organist may play over the chant for the psalm. The priest makes his way to the litany desk, and the psalm is begun when he is on his knees. If the playing of the chant will not occupy all the time taken by the priest to reach the litany desk, the organist may improvise for a few moments before giving out the chant.

In the American church, the Penitential Office begins with the psalm. The priest may be at the faldstool if the Litany has been said; otherwise, time must be allowed for him to proceed thither. The chant is given out at the conclusion of the Litany, Third Collect or hymn that precedes the Penitential Office.

Psalm 51 (*Miserere mei, Deus*) may be said, but it is generally chanted if the choir is present. An Anglican chant may be used (perhaps in a minor key); or the inflected and harmonized arrangement by Sir John Stainer, which has become traditional in many churches, may be sung.

The Lesser Litany ("Lord, have mercy upon us," etc.), the Lord's Prayer and the Responses may be intoned. The choirmaster whose service book does not contain music for the responses may procure a separate setting.

The two prayers which follow will be said on a note if the responses have been intoned.

The prayer beginning, "Turn thou us, O good Lord, and so shall we be turned," etc., may be said on a note, or the traditional inflected and harmonized setting may be used.

The prayer that follows (two prayers in the American book) may also be intoned.

The organist may improvise while the priest returns to the prayer desk or whatever place from which he will continue or close the service.

§11 Accession Service

(*In the English and Canadian churches only*)

The English and Canadian books contain "Forms of Prayer with Thanksgivings to Almighty God for use on the anniversary of the day of the accession of the reigning sovereign."

The first section provides substitutions and additions at the services of Morning and Evening Prayer.

Special Responses are used after the Creed (or after the second recital of the Lord's Prayer) and these are properly intoned.

An extra Collect (beginning, "O God, who providest for thy people," etc.) is intoned after the Collect for the day.

Three prayers are provided to be incorporated into the Litany, or read after the anthem or hymn which follows the Third Collect. In churches where intoning ceases after the Third Collect, these prayers will be said in the natural voice; elsewhere, they may properly be intoned.

The second section of the Accession Service consists of a Collect, Epistle and Gospel to be used at the Communion Service. If the anniversary of the accession falls upon a Sunday or Holy Day for which a collect, epistle and gospel are appointed, those contained in the Accession Service are not used, although the Collect may follow that of the day.

The third section provides a brief, alternative service. After the opening hymn, the Te Deum is chanted or sung to a festival setting, the Lord's Prayer is intoned, the Responses chanted in the traditional manner, and the balance of the service said or intoned.

§12 Dominion Day Service

(In the Canadian church only)

The form of service for Dominion Day and other occasions of national thanksgiving involves no substantial change in the order of the regular services. Proper psalms and lessons are appointed to be read instead of those that would ordinarily be used, and special prayers and thanksgivings are to be read in addition to or instead of those usually read after the Third Collect.

The appointed Collect is that of the Seventh Sunday after Trinity, and an Epistle and Gospel are also appointed.

§13 Children's Service

(*In the Canadian Prayer Book only*)

In some parishes it is the custom, on certain festivals, to have a children's service in the church, either at the hour usually set aside for Sunday School or at Morning Prayer.

Many clergymen prefer to follow the usual form of Morning or Evening Prayer with slight adaptations: others use the order of Service for Children found in the Prayer Book, especially if the service is held in place of Sunday School.

In selecting the music for such a service, the aim should be to train the children to the services of the church rather than to lower the service to a childish level. If the Sunday School is properly conducted, the children will be quite prepared for a church service.

After the opening hymn, the Sentences, Confession and Absolution as found in the Service for Children may be said. Since this first part of the service is somewhat informal, it should not be intoned.

However, in parishes where the responses are regularly chanted, they should be chanted at this service also.

There follows a psalm from the suggested list at the end of the service. This psalm should be chanted. Perhaps it might be taught to the children at Sunday School two or three weeks before the service in the church.

One Lesson is appointed to be read, and it is followed by the Jubilate Deo or some other canticle usually chanted after the Second Lesson.

The Creed and the Collects follow, and the service proceeds as at Morning or Evening Prayer unless the rector arranges otherwise.

§14 Service for Missions

(*In the Canadian Prayer Book only*)

The Special Service for Missions consists of substitutions for parts of the regular services of the church.

Appropriate Sentences are appointed to be read instead of those usually read at Morning or Evening Prayer. They may be said or intoned, according to the custom of the parish.

The Exhortation, Confession, Absolution, Lord's Prayer and Responses follow as usual; but at Morning Prayer, Psalm 96 may be chanted instead of the Venite.

Proper psalms and lessons are provided instead of those that would ordinarily be used at Morning or Evening Prayer. Substitute canticles are also appointed to be chanted after the lessons: *Cantate Domino* (Isaiah 42:10–12) after the First Lesson, and *Surge Illuminator* (passages from Isaiah 60) after the Second Lesson. Each canticle is followed by the Gloria Patri.

After the Creed, there is a short period for silent prayer, followed by the Responses. We know of no service book which contains a setting for these particular responses; nevertheless, they should be chanted. By following the pattern set in the responses for Morning and Evening Prayer, one should have no difficulty in arranging special responses in the traditional form.

After the Collect for the day, there follow three collects for missions.

An anthem or a hymn is sung; and the prayers that follow are substitutions for those ordinarily said or intoned.

A Collect, Epistle and Gospel are provided for use at a Communion Service; although if the service is held on a major church festival, it is probable that only the Collect for missions will be used, and that after the collect for the festival. Some of the prayers contained in this service may also be read after the Offertory or before the Benediction.

§15 Harvest Thanksgiving

(*In the Canadian Prayer Book only*)

In the Form of Thanksgiving for the Blessings of Harvest, as contained in the Canadian Prayer Book, only minor departures are made from the order of Morning or Evening Prayer.

Special Opening Sentences are appointed instead of those generally used, Psalm 147 may be chanted instead of the Venite at

Morning Prayer, proper psalms and lessons are provided, and there are several prayers which may be used after the Collect for the day and after the anthem (or hymn).

A Collect, Epistle and Gospel are provided for the Communion Service.

§16 Institution and Induction of Ministers

(In the Canadian and American Prayer Books only)

When a new rector is appointed to a parish, he is usually formally instituted or inducted by the bishop or someone (probably the archdeacon) acting for the bishop.

These services, of infrequent occurrence in any church, should be very carefully planned and rehearsed in order that they may proceed as smoothly and as naturally as the services that are held daily or weekly.

Both the Canadian and American Prayer Books make provision for a Service of Institution and Induction, and the organist and choirmaster will do well to become familiar with it. Since the two Prayer Books differ in the order of service, it may be well to consider them separately.

In the Canadian church, the Induction Service is usually combined with Morning or Evening Prayer, either of which proceeds as usual until the end of the Third Collect. The Prayer Book appoints proper psalms and lessons, and directs that the Collect for St. Simon and St. Jude's Day be read instead of that which would ordinarily be used as the Collect for the day.

After the Third Collect, an anthem or a hymn may be sung.

Then the bishop reads, in his natural speaking voice, the paragraph beginning, "Dearly beloved in the Lord," etc.; or, if the bishop is not present, his representative will read the bishop's mandate and the paragraph beginning, "Dearly beloved in the Lord, forasmuch as our well-beloved in Christ," etc.

There follows a short period of silent prayer. The organist should arrange with his rector beforehand a signal to be given when the silent prayer is to be ended. Having received the signal, the organist sounds the note of intonation.

The Lesser Litany ("Lord, have mercy upon us," etc.) may be intoned in unison or in harmony, accompanied or unaccompanied. The Lord's Prayer may be accompanied to maintain the pitch.

The Responses that follow should be intoned if it is the custom of the parish. Few service books contain the music for these responses, but they may be obtained or arranged. One bishop at least used to ask that a copy of the versicles and responses be sent to him in advance in order that he might not be taken unawares by a setting that was not standard or not familiar to him.

The three prayers following the responses will be intoned if the responses have been intoned.

Then follows the actual induction, during which there is no music. The organist's next duty will be to play the hymn after the induction, which will be announced.

The bishop then delivers several short exhortations concerning the duties of the minister. This may be done in the chancel, or at the various parts of the church at which the minister's duties are customarily performed.

No music is prescribed for this part of the service, but in one diocese the bishop has established the custom of singing appropriate stanzas of the hymn, "We love the place, O God" (their order rearranged), while he and the newly-inducted minister proceed from one part of the church to another. This serves the double purpose of providing an opportunity for the people to participate, and of avoiding awkward silences.

The hymn is announced, and while the bishop and the incumbent are proceeding to the font, the following stanzas are sung:

We love the place, O God,
  Wherein thine honor dwells;
The joy of thine abode
  All earthly joy excels.

We love the sacred font;
  For there the Holy Dove

To pour is ever wont
His blessings from above.

The bishop then reads the passage of Scripture and the Exhortation concerning baptism. When the incumbent has said: "I will so do, the Lord being my helper"; and as he and the bishop move towards the prayer desk, the following stanza is sung without announcement or delay:

It is the house of prayer,
Wherein thy servants meet;
And thou, O Lord, art there
Thy chosen flock to greet.

After the Exhortation and the incumbent's reply, a move is made to the lectern, and the people sing:

We love the word of life,
The word that tells of peace,
Of comfort in the strife,
And joys that never cease.

Since the Exhortations at both the lectern and the pulpit have to do with the presenting of the Word of God to the people, nothing is sung while the bishop and the incumbent proceed to the pulpit. As they leave the pulpit and make their way towards the altar, this stanza is sung:

We love thine altar, Lord:
O what on earth so dear?
For there, in faith adored,
We find thy presence near.

The bishop addresses his charge at the altar, and immediately turns to the people to remind them of their duties. As he concludes with the words: "Bear ye one another's burdens, and so fulfil the law of Christ"; the hymn may be completed:

We love to sing below
For mercies freely given;
But O, we long to know
The triumph-song of heaven.

Lord Jesus, give us grace
  On earth to love thee more,
In heaven to see thy face,
  And with thy saints adore.

A hymn or anthem may follow, the sermon is preached, and Morning or Evening Prayer proceeds as usual except that two prayers are appointed to be read before the Benediction.

It is not usual to combine an induction with a Communion Service, but if such a case arises, the induction may take place immediately after the opening hymn or after the Gospel. The proper Collect will be that for St. Simon and St. Jude's Day, and the Prayer Book appoints passages of Scripture to be read for the Epistle and the Gospel.

The Service of Institution in the American book is somewhat shorter. After the hymn, the bishop or his representative reads the paragraph beginning, "Dearly beloved in the Lord," etc., and the Letter of Institution. The keys of the church are then presented by the wardens and received by the incumbent.

A note may be given; and the versicle and response ("The Lord be with you; And with thy spirit"), the Lord's Prayer and the prayer that follows may be intoned.

The incumbent then enters the sanctuary and receives the Bible, the Prayer Book, and the Books of Canon from the bishop.

As soon as the bishop has said: "And be thou in all things a pattern to the flock committed to thy care," the organist will give out the chant for the psalm that follows—Psalm 68 or Psalm 26. At the conclusion of the Gloria Patri which ends the psalm, a note may be given, and all that follows may be intoned.

After the concluding prayer there may be a hymn, followed by the sermon. Morning or Evening Prayer will then be continued, or the Holy Communion will be celebrated, as usual.

§17 Laying of a Foundation Stone

(In the Canadian Prayer Book only)

There are organists and choirmasters, particularly those whose duties lie in long-established city parishes, who are never throughout their entire careers called upon to prepare services in connection with the building and consecration of a new church. It is a rare experience for any church musician, but one that is more likely to fall to the lot of organists and choirmasters in rural and suburban parishes where the church must expand to meet the needs of growing communities.

The Laying of a Foundation Stone is a great and historic event in the life of any parish, and the organist and choirmaster and choristers whose privilege it is to participate in such a service should spare no effort to make it a festival occasion.

There are many details to be planned in advance of the service. The arrangements are, primarily, the responsibility of the rector and wardens, but the organist and choirmaster should be kept informed so that he may make sure that suitable accommodation is made for him and the choir.

Generally, a platform is erected for the bishop and other clergy, and space should be reserved for the choir on or near the platform.

A piano is the most serviceable instrument for accompaniments. If the congregation does not own a piano, there should be no difficulty in renting or borrowing one providing that arrangements are made for its careful transportation. A small reed organ is more easily transported but its thin tones are lost in the open air.

It is well to submit complete plans for the service (including the setting for the responses) to the bishop for his approval or modification, so that there may be no confusing last-minute changes. The submission of plans will be made by the rector, of course, but the organist and choirmaster should see that the music is in the rector's hands in good time.

On the day of the service, the choir and clergy proceed in procession from the place where they have donned their vestments to the site of the new church. The procession must of necessity be silent, since facilities for music are lacking.

When the clergy have reached the platform and the choristers their places, the service will probably begin with a hymn.

At the conclusion of the hymn, the note of intonation will be sounded and the Sentences and Responses intoned.

Psalm 84 is then chanted. The piano is not a good instrument for accompanying chanting, but it will suffice if the choir is not prepared to chant the psalm without accompaniment.

The Lesson is read and, immediately following, the Jubilate Deo is chanted or a hymn sung.

A note is given, and the Versicles and Responses beginning, "Behold I lay in Sion a chief corner stone, elect, precious," etc., are intoned, as is the prayer following.

The corner stone is then laid, and at the conclusion of the paragraph which begins, "Here let true faith, the fear of God, and brotherly love ever remain," etc., the note of intonation is given for the Responses, the Lord's Prayer, and the three prayers that follow.

An address is usually made, which may or may not be preceded by a hymn, but will probably be followed by one. If the choir is equal to it and conditions are judged to be not too unfavorable, an anthem may be sung before or after the address.

The two prayers and the Benediction which close the service may be intoned or not, and a hymn may follow.

At the conclusion of the service, the procession will re-form and return to the place where the clergy and choir are to doff their vestments.

§18 Consecration of a Church or Chapel

(In the Canadian and American Prayer Books only)

On the day on which the church is to be consecrated, the clergy, wardens and choir assemble inside the main entrance, the church officials being nearest the door and the choir formed ready for the procession.

Before and while the officials assemble, the organist may play a voluntary as usual.

The bishop, his chaplain and attendants approach the main door from the outside, and are received by the rector and wardens. Arrangements should be made for someone to signal the organist when the bishop reaches the door, so that the music may cease.

After a brief ceremony at the entrance, another signal should be given to the organist who will then play over the chant for the psalm. At the first sound of the organ, the procession moves slowly up the main aisle.

The Prayer Books direct that the bishop alone shall chant alternate verses of the psalm, the other verses being taken by the choir and people. However, most bishops prefer that the entire psalm be chanted by all present.

If the procession is not ended when the psalm has been chanted, the organist may improvise until the bishop has taken his place in the sanctuary.

Then the instruments of donation and endowment are presented, after which the bishop says, in his natural speaking voice: "Dearly beloved in the Lord, forasmuch as devout and holy men," etc.; and as he concludes with the words: "Let us faithfully and devoutly beg his blessing on this our undertaking (and say)," the note of intonation may be sounded.

The several prayers that follow should be intoned in parishes where intoning is the custom.

The Sentence of Consecration is then read and is followed, in the American church only, by the prayer beginning, "Blessed be thy Name, O Lord," etc.

A hymn will probably be sung, and the regular service for the day will follow. If the service is that of Morning or Evening Prayer, proper psalms and lessons will be used, and a special Collect will be read instead of that which would ordinarily be used on that day. In the Canadian church, the prayer beginning, "Blessed be thy Name, O Lord," etc., is read after the General Thanksgiving.

If there is a celebration of the Holy Communion, the proper

Collect, Epistle and Gospel as contained in the Service of Consecration are used.

A prayer is appointed to be read before the Benediction.

§19 Organ Recitals and Other Musical Services

Most churches permit recitals and performances of choral works provided that they are conducted with reverence and decorum. Clergymen who refuse permission for recitals may have unpleasant memories of musicians who mistook the church for a concert hall, or may realize all too well what can happen when an organist and choirmaster with no sense of the fitness of things is given a free rein. When one's musical ambitions are thwarted by objections on the part of the rector, it is only fair to remember that he is responsible for safeguarding the dignity and reverence of the church, and that he is quite justified in being cautious.

The performance of music in the church should be undertaken as a *service*, as an offering to God of the fruits of one of His most glorious gifts to mankind. This motive, which may well be explained to the congregation, need not lessen the listeners' enjoyment of the music—on the contrary, their pleasure should be the greater. If the musician cannot think of his playing or singing as an act of praise and worship, he should abandon all thought of a recital or plan to have it elsewhere; for the church is dedicated to the praise and worship of God, and nothing else.

If there is a printed programme, names of performers and composers should be included solely as means of identification. The musicians should be regarded as agents of God in the practice of their art; and surely this is sufficient glory and satisfaction for any man! It should not be necessary to say that applause is out of place in church.

If the organist is playing a recital, it is suggested that he enter the church quietly, adopting for the occasion the demeanor of a servant rather than that of a *maestro.* He will do well to wear his cassock, and perhaps his surplice also if his rector so advises.

The recital may begin without preliminaries, or, if the rector is present, a prayer or two may be said.

If the organist feels it necessary to make remarks during the recital, he should ask permission of the rector beforehand. Remarks should concern the music itself, and should not constitute a glorification of the composers. When the programme includes Minuets, Gavottes, Sarabandes, etc., it is advisable to remind the congregation that, while these terms were at one time applied to dances, they are now used to designate styles and forms of musical compositions. Without such an explanation some people might find it difficult to reconcile what they consider light music with the atmosphere of reverence that should prevail in church.

If there is a soloist in addition to the organist, he or she should enter the church quietly with the organist and take a place in the choir stalls. Unless the words of the solos are contained in the Bible, the Prayer Book, or the hymnal officially sanctioned by the church, they should be submitted to the rector for his approval.

On no account should the soloist sing with his or her back towards the sanctuary. If the soloist is a violinist or a 'cellist, perhaps it would be well to confine vestments to a cassock, since the wide sleeves of a surplice might prove troublesome. The player of a bowed instrument can scarcely play in the choir stalls and a more convenient location must be found—not in the middle of the choir, however.

Choral performances of oratorios, cantatas, or miscellaneous programmes of anthems, motets or carols may be described aptly as Services of Praise. The choristers should be vested, of course, and should enter and leave the church in their usual manner.

It is better to begin the service with a hymn and some prayers. A shortened form of Evening Prayer may well precede the programme, and the Offertory, the Benediction and a hymn may close the service.

Sometimes a Service of Praise is sung by an augmented choir, or by combined choirs. Whatever the seating problem, no choristers should be permitted to sit or stand with their backs towards the sanctuary.

It is unlikely that the parish organist and choirmaster will have to prepare services not mentioned in these pages. There are other services in the Prayer Books, but some of them (for instance, the Visitation of the Sick) are held in private; while others (such as Ordinations) are nearly always held in cathedrals whose organists and choirmasters require no assistance from a manual such as this.

V · EQUIPMENT AND ORGANIZATION

§1 The Organ

Organists and choirmasters generally have to be content with whatever equipment they find in the church when they begin their duties. However, renovations are sometimes made; and, since we have presumed that the organist and choirmaster may have to prepare services for the Laying of a Foundation Stone and the Consecration of a Church, we may presume also that, in the normal sequence of events, he may find himself provided with new equipment. Whether or not he is fortunate enough to be the beneficiary of a renovation or a new building, he should be prepared to make any possible and reasonable changes that will lead to better results in his work.

The most important and expensive item of equipment is the organ. If the instrument is poor, inadequate, worn out or badly situated, the best way to have it replaced or rebuilt is to work for the best possible results with it as it stands. Congregations will do their best towards providing suitable equipment for a hard and capable worker; they are less likely to go to trouble and expense for a slovenly musician who shirks his work in the hope of forcing the congregation to provide better equipment. In the latter case the result is likely to be a new organist rather than a new organ.

If a fairly large organ is to be installed, few problems will arise. The difficulty of securing balance decreases as the ranks of pipes increase, and it will seldom be necessary to modify the specifications of a reputable builder.

It is the small two-manual organ, such as is purchased for hundreds of churches with limited funds and space, which will require forethought. Many such instruments, which should be adequate in size for the churches that house them, lose much of their potential efficiency through an unwise selection of stops. This, let us hasten to say, is not always the fault of the builders, who are harassed by organists and committees to provide "fancy stops" which should never be included in the specifications.

One serious oversight is the failure to remember that the organ must be a suitable instrument for accompanying the choir. The typical small two-manual organ has a specification something like the following:

SWELL—Aeoline 8′
Gamba 8′
Stopped Diapason 8′
Flute 4′
Oboe 8′
GREAT—Open Diapason 8′
Melodia 8′
Dulciana 8′
Flute 4′
PEDAL—Bourdon 16′
Lieblich Gedacht 16′

Such an organ, properly equipped with couplers, serves very well for accompanying congregational singing. It is not very satisfactory for accompanying anthems sung by small choirs, the psalms, responses, etc. Foundation tone—that is, diapason stops—should be available for accompaniments, and the open diapason on the Great Organ is (or should be) much too strong for this purpose.

This defect may be overcome either by having a softer open diapason on the Swell or, better still, by enclosing the Great Organ in a swell box of its own. It is surprising that the suggestion to enclose the Great Organ so often meets with opposition. It solves a very vexing problem, and has the added advantage of rendering a comparatively large section of the organ subject to expression.

It is desirable to include on the Swell Organ a much softer flute stop than is generally provided. The aeoline is serviceable for soft playing during the Communion, at weddings, etc., but it tends to become monotonous if it is the only stop available for that use. A very soft flute that can be used alone or with the aeoline lends at least a little variety.

If one cannot have both a reed stop and a moderately voiced diapason on the Swell Organ, the open diapason should certainly be chosen. In lieu of a reed, the gamba may be so voiced that it adds pungency to the full Swell and may be used also as a solo stop. When the oboe is included, it should be voiced with regard to its general utility rather than as a stop to be used exclusively for solo work.

Such an arrangement will provide a solid background for a small choir without overpowering it, and will also contribute much to the volume when the swell box is opened.

The Great Organ, if it must be limited to four ranks of pipes, may well conform to the specification given above. While unification is generally frowned upon, it does seem advantageous to provide some means of playing certain stops of the Swell Organ from the Great manual. For instance, if one wishes to use the stopped diapason or four-foot flute as a solo stop, the gamba or aeoline might provide a better accompaniment than the Great dulciana. On most organs such a combination is impossible, since the gamba and the stopped diapason cannot be used both simultaneously and independently. The provision of knobs or tablets which will enable the organist to use certain stops of the Swell Organ with and independently of the others can scarcely be termed unification in the usual sense of the word, and it will add much to the resources of a small instrument.

A Pedal section of two stops is insufficient for even a small organ. There are many times when the bourdon is too strong for a manual combination, and the lieblich gedacht too weak. Moreover, both stops are of much the same quality, and some small variety in the quality of the tone is desirable to relieve monotony.

The lieblich gedacht is often an extension of the Swell stopped diapason—that is to say, a lower octave is added to the stopped diapason and the lieblich gedacht becomes, in effect, a coupler. If funds do not permit the addition of independent Pedal stops, the principle of extension may be applied beneficially to other manual stops—the gamba, and perhaps the open diapason. This or any other means of gaining string tone and a bright, strongly-voiced stop will prove a boon to the organist.

Our small two-manual organ may, with very little added expense, be made up as follows:

SWELL—Open Diapason 8′
Gamba 8′
Aeoline 8′
Lieblich Gedacht 8′
Stopped Diapason 8′
Stopped Flute 4′
Oboe 8′ (voiced as a general purpose stop)

GREAT (enclosed)—
Open Diapason 8′
Dulciana 8′
Melodia 8′
Flute 4′
Gamba 8′ (from Swell Organ)
Aeoline 8′ (from Swell Organ)
Oboe 8′ (from Swell Organ)

PEDAL—Bourdon 16′
Lieblich Gedacht 16′ (extension from Swell Stopped Diapason)
Gamba 16′ (extension from Swell)
Open Diapason 16′ (extension from Great).

COUPLERS—
Swell Sub
Swell Super
Great Sub
Great Super
Swell to Great Sub
Swell to Great Unison
Swell to Great Super
Swell to Pedal Unison

Swell to Pedal Super
Great to Pedal

Extensions and borrowings are not recommended when independent ranks of pipes can be afforded, but they are justified as a means of extending the resources of a small instrument.

A specification such as that outlined above should not be considered as an ideal—much more could be added without incurring the charge of extravagance!—but it can prove adequate if it is the best that the congregation can afford. When funds permit the addition of more stops, a four-foot principal on the Great or Swell should be the first consideration, and attention should be given to building up the general *ensemble* rather than to solo stops. One can imagine nothing more irritating than the gift of a clarinet or a vox humana or, worst of all, chimes as an addition to a very small organ. Solo stops are very nice and desirable, but they are expensive luxuries on small instruments that lack a solid, balanced foundation. Chimes are merely a nuisance to the organist, and efforts should be made to persuade prospective donors to invest their money in something more useful.

Some congregations, although desirous of providing better equipment for their organists, cannot afford pipe organs, especially when their purchase would entail alterations to the church buildings for their accommodation. Time was when only reed instruments of the melodeon and harmonium types were available as substitutes for organs. They were never satisfactory, and their use was governed by necessity rather than choice. Today, these makeshifts have been rendered nearly obsolete by the electronic organ.

Electronic instruments are so often heard under unfavorable conditions in places other than churches that a prejudice against them has arisen in the minds of many people. Perhaps the majority of organists regard them with disfavor, although even among organists condemnation is by no means unanimous.

While one would hesitate to make a general recommendation of the electronic organ in preference to the small pipe organ, the fact remains that the electronic will be considered by the committees of many small churches, whether the organist likes it or not. Furthermore, where funds are low and space limited, the electronic organ may be considered as an alternative, not for a pipe organ, but for a glorified harmonium or nothing at all.

The organist who plays a tiny, two-manual pipe organ may yearn, at times, for a three- or four-manual instrument; but, if he is wise, he makes the most of what he has. Similarly, the man who is asked to play an electronic organ may dream of all the things that he could do with a pipe organ, but he has really no grounds for self-pity. Compared with many of his colleagues who still have to play worn-out, inadequate little pipe organs or reed instruments, he is fortunate.

In an earlier chapter we spoke of the splendid results that can be achieved by a choirmaster who accepts conditions as they are and makes the most of his resources. The same can be said of an organist. Asked to play an instrument other than that of his choice, his first step should be to remove all prejudice from his mind, and to concentrate upon the possibilities of the instrument rather than dwell on its limitations. For, after all, the effect of an instrument depends largely upon the skill and judgement of the person who plays it. An organist with little of either skill or judgement can produce terrible effects from the finest organ: an experienced player can do good work with almost any kind of instrument. Thus, without attempting to minimize the differences that do exist between pipe organs and electronic instruments, we must recognize that popular opinion is influenced by the fact that pipe organs are more often than not played by capable organists, while electronic instruments, especially those heard over the radio, are often manipulated by people who do not know how to use them well.

The electronic organ is giving satisfactory service in many churches. It provides more variety of tone quality than does a small pipe organ. Many solo effects are quite beautiful; flute and string tone, separately and in combination, is good. In striving for diapason and chorus reed tone, care must be exercised, but results are as satisfactory as those obtained from a small pipe organ.

One distinct advantage of the electronic organ is the wide range of volume. The same full tone that is used for accompanying congregational singing is available for the accompaniment of anthems and solos: a touch of the amplifying pedal reduces the volume instantly. Another important consideration is the fact that the electronic instrument is never out of tune and requires practically no servicing.

Two precautions must be taken in installing an electronic organ:

First, a small chamber should be provided for the tone cabinet. Results are seldom satisfactory when the tone cabinet is in the church or facing into the church. One would imagine that the people who install the organ would be careful of this detail, but they seldom are.

Second, the tone cabinet (or cabinets) should be capable of producing more volume than is required or desirable for the church. Harshness and a metallic quality will be noticed if the organ has to be pushed to its limits.

One eminent organist who has read these pages thinks that too much has been said about the electronic organ—that we should assume the pipe organ as the only instrument suitable for church music. However, we feel that it would be idle to ignore the existence of electronic organs; or to pretend that organists who read these pages may never have to play them. And, if we are to recognize them at all, we must, without necessarily recommending them, be honest enough to acquaint the organists with their advantages under certain conditions as well as with their disadvantages.

The organ proper—that is, the pipes or, in the case of an electronic instrument, the tone cabinets—should be situated near the choir in order that they may benefit from its support. If the choir stalls are in the chancel it is advisable to divide the organ, the Great and Pedal being on one side of the chancel and the Swell on the other. If the opening and closing hymns are sung in procession, and if the organ is large enough to warrant further division, a few ranks of pipes may be situated near the place where the procession begins or ends.

A very important consideration is the location of the console, particularly if the organist is also the choirmaster. With the passing of the old tracker action, it is no longer necessary for the organist to sit near the pipes where he can neither see his choristers nor be seen by them.

The organist should be able to see from the console, either directly or with the aid of a mirror, the sanctuary, the prayer desk, the entire choir, and the main entrance to the nave. He should be in full view of the clergy and the choir. This happy state of affairs does not always exist, and the work of the choir suffers in consequence.

In many churches the console is situated in a space appropriated from that designed for the choir stalls. The organist can see the choristers on the opposite side of the chancel and, perhaps, a few on his own side; and a mirror inconspicuously placed may bring within his view the images of those choristers whom he cannot see directly.

An admirable place for the console is in the nave, in a space provided by shortening two or three of the front pews. From this point beside the center aisle the organist can not only see his choir, but he can hear them and the organ to the best advantage. Admittedly in the case of a large organ, this situation might make the console and the organist so prominent that the attention of people sitting near by would be distracted. A small console, however, may be lowered into a shallow well let into the floor, and a suitable screen placed behind the bench will conceal the organist from the congregation.

The whole problem would be solved if the console could be placed in the middle of the choir, but no church officials would permit that location, nor would the organist desire it.

There should be, within easy reach of the organ bench, a cupboard or shelf for books and music. And a back rest on the bench will be greatly appreciated by the organist during those brief periods when he has nothing to do.

§2 The Choir Stalls

Since choristers spend more time in church than most members of the congregation, it is not too much to ask that they be provided with comfortable seats. Most choir pews, especially those occupied by the boys, are too high and, as a result, there is bound to be some fidgeting.

The pews should be far enough apart to permit the choristers to stand comfortably without rubbing their shins on the kneeling benches or the backs of their legs against the pews. For practical purposes, it is well to have each pew on a slightly higher level than the one in front of it.

Kneeling benches should be securely fastened, and so placed that the choristers can kneel erect. Nothing looks worse than kneeling choristers partly supported by the edges of their pews, and such a posture is detrimental to good breathing. The kneeling benches should be padded, or at least covered with carpeting. Choristers have to kneel for long periods, and they should not be distracted from their duties by aching knees.

The provision for books and music merits some attention. A narrow trough fastened to the back of the pew ahead is not a suitable receptacle for music. The chorister who, while standing, has to reach for another book must fumble awkwardly, and his attention is taken from the choirmaster. Moreover, the troughs are hard on music, resulting in creased and wrinkled pages of hymn and service books, and anthems crumpled beneath the weight of heavier volumes. Unless the trough fits snugly to the back of the pew (and few of them do!) sheet music will be on the floor more often than not.

The ideal provision for music is a sloping desk or board about eight inches wide, and with a narrow ledge to prevent books from slipping off, fastened to the pew in front. It permits the chorister to find his places well in advance, and to have his books where they are visible and readily accessible. Sloping desks can easily be added to stalls which are not already provided with them, and they are well worth the trouble and slight expense.

§3 Vestments

Vestments usually worn by Anglican choristers are the cassock and surplice or cotta.

The cassock is a fairly close-fitting garment that reaches to within about two inches of the floor. Choristers' cassocks are usually single-breasted, buttoned their full length.

In most churches the cassocks are black, but there is no reason why they should be. Scarlet or blue cassocks are often worn, and purple is the accepted color for cathedrals. More and more choirs are abandoning funereal black, and the question of color is one worthy of consideration when new cassocks are to be ordered.

The organist will be more comfortable in a double-breasted cassock whose fuller skirt allows more freedom of movement for pedalling. It is generally worn with a cincture or girdle. Double-breasted cassocks are proper for choristers, also, but they are considerably more expensive than single-breasted garments.

The cassock is worn whenever the chorister is in the chancel, whether at a service or a rehearsal, or merely to distribute music or post numbers on the hymn board.

The surplice is a white linen, loosely-fitting garment with wide sleeves, worn over the cassock. Some leeway is permitted in the style of surplices: some are quite voluminous, others can only be described as skimpy; some are plain at the top, others are gathered. A happy medium is a surplice that reaches nearly to the knees, and whose sleeves allow a narrow band of the cassock sleeve to show.

The cotta, worn instead of the surplice, is generally shorter than the surplice, with elbow-length sleeves and a square rather than a round neck. Sometimes, especially for servers, the sleeves and bottom are trimmed with lace, but choristers' cottas are seldom thus adorned.

Organists are advised to wear surplices with either elbow-length sleeves or split sleeves that will fall back out of the way when they are playing. Most clerical outfitters supply specially tailored vestments for organists.

The surplice is always worn at church services, and at no other time. It is most improper for a choir to be surpliced for a concert in the parish hall or elsewhere.

In some churches the choir is not surpliced for services on Good Friday, a custom which is inconsistent with church tradition and for which no reasonable explanation seems to be given.

The cost of providing cassocks and surplices is a real burden to many small parishes, and a compromise is sometimes reached by having the vestments made by the women of the church. The choice of women to do the work should be governed by their competence rather than their willingness. A good pattern should be obtained and, if possible, one person should cut all the material to pattern.

Since women of the choir seldom have occasion to appear without surplices, economy is sometimes effected by substituting a plain skirt and dicky for the cassock. Occasionally one sees women choristers with cape-like garments that serve as surplices, but this substitution is not recommended.

Generally speaking, vestments supplied by clerical outfitters wear better, are styled more correctly and retain their good appearance longer than homemade garments. If funds are available for the purchase of material, it would be wise, before deciding to have the vestments made by the women of the parish, to consider very carefully the possibilities of increasing the funds to the extent of purchasing tailor-made vestments.

Many years ago, when stocks and ruffs were normal neckwear for men and boys, a uniform appearance was achieved with cassocks and surplices as the only extra garments for church use. In these days, however, when every man and boy in the choir is likely to turn up with a different-colored shirt collar and tie, it is desirable to supply some form of neckwear that will serve as a standard—unless, of course, the necks of the cassocks are cut very high.

Eton collars, extensively used for boy choristers, were quite practical at one time when they were part of the boys' ordinary dress, but they are not so practical today. Their use necessitates making a buttonhole in the back of the cassock neck, and there is nothing to fasten them to or hold them in place at the front. When left in the choir room to be put on just before the service, they are apt to become smudged and dented; and most boys are so anxious to get away after church that they rip off the collars to the detriment of the buttonholes. However, if they can be laundered weekly and replaced often, Eton collars do lend a neat appearance to the boys. Ties should be worn with them.

The only alternative form of neckwear seems to be the ruff, and a very sensible and comfortable alternative it is. It adds much to the boys' appearance, requires less careful handling, launders easily, and does not require that the cassock be mutilated by a buttonhole. There was a time when we should have thought it unnecessary to mention that ruffs button at the back, but after seeing one or two choirs whose ruff buttons were very conspicuously at the front, it seems wise to note the correct use.

If the boys wear ruffs, there is no reason why the men should not wear them, too; but it may take some tact and persuasion to get them to do so. If they remain obdurate, one can only try to persuade them to wear white shirt collars and quiet ties.

Women choristers often wear Eton collars, although the kindest thing that can be said about them is that they are not becoming. If the boys wear Eton collars, soft white collars about two inches wide that will lie flat are most suitable for the women. If the boys wear ruffs, uniformity will be preserved by having the women wear ruching of a width considered suitable. The combination of ruffs on the boys and Eton collars on the women is incongruous.

When there are women in the choir, the matter of headgear must be considered. Mortar board caps are popular, although they were not designed for such use and soon become shabby at the corners unless carefully handled. Skull caps may be quaint or ridiculous, depending upon who is wearing them. Canterbury caps are neat, long-wearing and comfortable.

In some choirs merit badges are worn by boys who earn them. They consist of a cross or some other appropriate symbol suspended from the neck by a ribbon. The wearing of merit badges should be an honor reserved for those who have given long and valuable service to the choir.

§4 Books

It is recommended that separate copies of all books, anthems, services, etc. be furnished each member of the choir.

Hymn books for choir use should, of course, contain the tunes. Some hymnals are published in a "melody edition"—i. e., only the soprano, or the soprano and alto parts are given—and these, being cheaper than the complete edition, will serve very well for the women and boys. Never permit the sopranos to sing "by ear" from hymn books containing only the words.

Choristers should be asked to report loose or torn pages in order that repairs may be made promptly. A hymn book with one or two pages missing is useless. When bindings wear it is advisable to have the books rebound by a good workman. Rebound hymnals are often more durable than new ones.

Equally important is the Prayer Book, which every chorister should be taught to use. Editions which will remain open when left on the music rack are to be preferred: a book that closes when it is set down makes it necessary for the user to find his place whenever he wishes to refer to it. Attached bookmarks are a convenience, enabling the chorister to find in advance places which do not appear in their regular order in the service, such as the collect, epistle and gospel.

Choristers should be required to follow in the Prayer Book all parts of the service not contained in their psalters and service books. In some churches each chorister supplies his or her own Prayer Book, which thus becomes a personal and cherished possession.

Most psalters are published in at least two editions—with and without chants. Those which have a chant printed above each psalm are convenient if one is satisfied with the chants that are provided; but if alternative chants are to be used, it is a distinct disadvantage to have to refer to another part of the book. Generally speaking, the best edition for the choir is that which contains the words only. When chanting psalms, the chants have to be sung from memory in order that one's whole attention may be given to the words. If it is necessary to refer to the notes occasionally, a chant book on the music desk is as convenient as anything else. The organist will appreciate an edition of the psalter with larger type if one is available.

Most Anglican hymnals contain a section devoted to chants, responses, etc., which will serve the needs of the average parish choir. If more variety is desired, a selection may be made from the large number of excellent chant books that are available. Care should be taken to select a book which has not only attractive chants, but also the greatest number of other settings that may be useful.

It is a good plan to have a set of small manuscript books in which may be entered chants, tunes, occasional services, etc., which are not found in other books. It is neither legal nor honest to make manuscript copies of copyrighted material which is offered for sale by publishers.

A number should be allotted to each chorister, and that number should appear on the cover of his hymn book, psalter, chant book and manuscript book. If he knows that his books are reserved for his own use and that he is responsible for their good condition, he will take better care of them than might otherwise be the case.

While sets of anthem and services should be given catalogue numbers, too much inconvenience and loss of time would result from marking individual copies with the choristers' numbers. The organist's copies should be reserved for his own use, as he may have marked registration and other notes in them. Choristers should be urged not to fold or roll music.

Descants, faux bourdons, carols, etc., which are published separately on small sheets are difficult to manage. If possible, several of them should be bound together to form one small volume. One choir which uses descants at every service has five volumes of them. In order to avoid either carrying two or three books into church or confining the day's descants to one volume, the five have been bound into one book. The expense of binding has been justified by the added convenience, and by the ease with which the music is kept clean and fresh.

The organist should have two psalters and two copies of each anthem and service set aside for his own use. It is sometimes awkward to remove a hand from the manual when the bottom of a page is reached, and with two copies the organist can choose convenient places to turn pages. He should also have an extra hymn book when alternative tunes are used, or when hymns and chants are contained in the same volume. The organist's books should be sufficiently worn that they will stay open on the music rack.

§5 Service Lists

It is most important that the choristers know exactly what they are to sing, and how and when to sing it. In order that they may be fully informed and prepared for everything beforehand, a service list or programme is a necessity. Some churches have a printed order of service; but this is not sufficient, since the choir needs more directions than would appear on a form compiled for congregational use.

A typewritten or mimeographed list is, perhaps, the most satisfactory since the form can be altered to meet the needs of any and all services.

The following is a sample of such a list used by a small parish choir:

ST. JAMES' CHURCH

November 1, 19—
ALL SAINTS' DAY

HOLY COMMUNION

Hymn 398 – Tune: "Lasst uns erfreuen"
Descant (#10) verse 3
Introit: "The Souls of the righteous"
– – Chant 139 HB
Communion Service in D – – – – Piggott
(except where noted)
Kyrie
Gloria Tibi: page 933 HB
Gradual: Hymn 208 – Tune: "All Saints"
Gratias Tibi: page 933 HB
Credo
Anthem: – "What are these" – Stainer
Sermon
Offertory Hymn 215 – Tune: "Wiltshire"
Descant (#31) verses 3 and 5
Offertory Sentence 180 HB
Sursum Corda: page 935 HB
Sanctus
Benedictus qui venit
Agnus Dei
Communion Hymn 229 – Tune: "Picardy"
Pater Noster (Monotoned)
Gloria in Excelsis
Amen
Hymn 209 – Tune: "Pro omnibus sanctis"

EVENING PRAYER

Hymn 629 – – – – – – – Tune: "Alford"
Ferial Responses
Psalms CXLV, CXLVI – page 300 in Psalter
Chants 74, 78 CB
Magnificat 82 CB
Nunc Dimittis 101 CB
Anthem: "Souls of the Righteous" – Noble
Hymn 610 – – – – – – Tune: "Southwell"
Descant (#97) verses 2 and 4
Sermon
Offertory Hymn 216 – Tune: "Beatitudo"
Offertory Sentence 180 HB
Vesper Hymn 38 – – Tune: "St. Peter"
Hymn 619 – – – Tune: "Palms of Glory"

PRACTICES

Boys: Tuesday 4.30 p.m.
Friday 7.30 p.m.
Adults: Friday 8 p.m.

The above is not only a sample of a convenient service list, but might be regarded also as a good choice of music for a small, well-trained choir. The hymns on the list are as follows:

398	"Ye watchers and ye holy ones"
208	"Who are these like stars appearing"
215	"Give me the wings of faith, to rise"
229	"Let all mortal flesh keep silence"
209	"For all the saints who from their labors rest"
629	"Ten thousand times ten thousand"
610	"Jerusalem my happy home"
216	"How bright these glorious spirits shine"
38	"The Lord be with us as we bend"
619	"Palms of glory, raiment bright"

The descants at the communion service were by Geoffrey Shaw, from *The Descant Hymn Tune Book, No. 1;* that at the evening service was by T. W. Hanforth, from *The Sheffield Cathedral Descants, First Set.*

The anthem "Souls of the Righteous" was the composer's four-part arrangement.

The abbreviation HB after a number indicates that it is to be found in the back of the hymn book; CB refers the choristers to a separate chant book.

If preparing a typewritten list is found to be too troublesome, a good alternative is an inexpensive printed form listing the parts of the service used in the parish, and leaving blank spaces for writing in the numbers. The most convenient form is not more than five inches wide in order that it may be carried in the hymn book; and for that reason, it is preferable to have two forms, one for Holy Communion and Evening Prayer, the other for Morning Prayer and Evening Prayer. If the forms are in pads, carbon paper may be used and several filled in at one time. The following is a suitable form:

†

St. James' Church

Date____

Church Calendar

MORNING PRAYER	EVENING PRAYER
Hymn Descant verses	Hymn Descant verses
Responses	Responses
Invitatory	Psalms Page in Psalter Chants
Venite	Magnificat Cantate Domino Bonum est
Psalms Page in Psalter Chants	Nunc Dimittis Deus misereatur
Te Deum Benedictus es Benedicite	Anthem
Benedictus Jubilate	Hymn Descant verses
Anthem	Offertory Hymn Descant verses
Hymn Descant verses	Offertory Sentence
Offertory Hymn Descant verses	Amen Vesper Hymn
Offertory Sentence	Hymn Descant verses
Amen	
Hymn Descant verses	

PRACTICES FOR THE WEEK – Boys
Men

The spaces for descants may be left blank when they are not used; and where two or more canticles are listed, pencil marks will strike out those not required.

§6 The Choir Vestry

Vestment racks, music cupboards, chairs, and a table for the use of the librarian should be provided in a room set apart for the use of the choir; or, if such a room is not available, in some part of the building where they will not be disturbed.

Accommodation for vestments may range from an expensive cupboard with a separate compartment for each chorister, to a simple wooden or mental frame provided with hooks and garment hangers. Immoveable hooks are to be preferred to long rods on which hangers are suspended, for the long rods make it too easy for the careless chorister to slide his own or another's vestments away from their proper places. Over the racks should be two boards some nine inches wide, one about four inches above the other; and the space between these boards may be divided into compartments, each large enough to hold a hymn book, a psalter and a chant book. The rack used by women choristers should have extra compartments for headgear.

Much confusion will be avoided if a number is assigned to each compartment and the hook beneath it, and if all books and vestments which are to be kept in that place are marked with the same number. By such an arrangement, each chorister knows exactly where to find his own books and vestments, and there need be no last-minute searches for equipment.

If the racks are not enclosed, a cloth large enough to cover them should be obtained. It can be placed over the racks after services and practices, and removed completely before each session of the choir.

The ideal cupboard for music is one that consists of compartments about seven and one quarter inches wide, ten and one quarter inches deep, and of a height depending upon the number of copies it is to contain. Each compartment will hold one set of anthems.

If compartments cannot be provided, there should at least be some wooden shelves on which the anthems may be stored in numbered envelops. A catalogue of anthems should be kept, showing the seasonal classification and the numbers of the compartments or envelops in which they are to be found. Larger compartments may be provided for cantatas, etc.

If the choir room is not large enough to contain chairs for the whole choir, seating should be arranged elsewhere—in the parish hall or in a corridor. Discarded pews with numbered places are excellent accommodation for the choir before services.

The librarian's table should be furnished with a drawer containing scissors, a ruler, paste, and strips of paper for mending music. Business machine rolls are good for mending. Gummed paper makes neat repairs, but it is likely to dry out and peel in time.

The choir room should be dry and warm. Nothing causes more damage to vestments and music than dampness; nothing is more discouraging to choristers than a chilly vestry.

§7 The Practice Room

Choir practices should seldom be held in church if there is any other place to have them. The organ is a poor instrument for rehearsals, far inferior to the clear, precise notes of the piano. Moreover, the organ console is often in such a position that the organist-choirmaster cannot easily converse with and give directions to the choir from the organ bench.

There are times, of course, when it is desirable to have a final rehearsal in the church; but the real work of learning the music should have been done beforehand, leaving only the finishing touches to be added in the church. Experience will soon convince any choirmaster that his singers learn more easily, quickly and thoroughly when a piano is used at rehearsals.

Another strong objection to having rehearsals in the church is the difficulty in maintaining reverence. A certain degree of informality is expected at rehearsals, and the choirmaster should be free to banter or scold as the occasion dictates. The church is for worship only, and any levity serves to undermine the reverence that the choristers should have for the house of God.

Most choirs can arrange to have rehearsals in some part of the parish hall where there is a piano. The place should be well-lighted and comfortable, and should be reserved for the choir's use at regular practice times. The choirmaster has a perfect right to complain loudly and insistently when he hears of an entertainment or a meeting of some other church organization planned for the time and place of choir practice. There are enough outside activities to tempt the less devoted choir members without setting up competition within the church.

§8 Finances

The ideal way to purchase new books, music and vestments is to have an annual budget approved by the church officials. Some choirmasters are permitted to order what they require and turn the accounts over to the wardens for payment. Unfortunately, the problem of financing the choir is seldom so simply and conveniently solved in small parish churches.

Members of the choir who carry out their duties faithfully should not be asked to contribute more of their time and services: yet, if more financial assistance is required than the wardens can afford, the choristers must devise some means of supplying the lack or have their work hampered because of insufficient equipment.

Sooner or later in most choirs, the question of a membership fee is raised. Such a suggestion should be speedily and thoroughly discouraged. There is no more reason for the chorister to pay for his own equipment than there is for the rector to supply his own pulpit or the sexton his own brooms. Moreover, it is an embarrassing situation for a choirmaster who has just persuaded someone to join the choir to have to break the news that the recruit is expected to pay for the privilege.

It is a good plan first to give the people an opportunity to contribute to the support of the choir. Envelops marked "Choir Fund" may be distributed, and the need explained either by the rector or by a statement printed on the envelops. In many cases, no further appeal or effort is required.

If contributions fail, the choir might prepare a number of anthems, solos, etc. and hold a Service of Praise, arranging with the wardens that the offertory go to the choir fund. A carol service near Christmas would be an excellent means of adding to the fund.

A Service of Praise by another choir, perhaps one from a near-by city church, might be sponsored by the choir. Most church musicians are willing to lend assistance to another parish, and such an occasion could be made an inspiration and pleasure for one's own people.

In a small community where good concerts are rare, the choir can often arrange recitals by visitors. One has to be very careful that the expense of such a project does not equal or exceed the proceeds, and that the recital will be of good quality. A choir is judged not only by its own work but also by the work of others who perform under its auspices.

A committee within the choir, composed of people with some imagination and business sense, can think of many ways to meet the financial problems.

The choirmaster is warned, however, that he will probably have to do most of the work connected with any scheme that may be decided upon.

§9 Organization

If the choir is financially supported by the church, there is no real need for elected officers. Too many officers and committees can be a hindrance, wasting time that should be devoted to rehearsals on lengthy meetings and discussions. One of the greatest dangers is the "social committee" which, in its zeal to justify its existence, is apt to overdo its part. The choir is a working group, not a social club; and, while a little party is an excellent thing once in a while, it should not be considered part of the choir's programme or be permitted to interfere with rehearsals.

The average choir has very little business to transact—nothing that cannot be brought to the members' attention by the choirmaster (who will be anxious to get on with the rehearsal!) and speedily disposed of.

If the choir must raise funds for its own support, the election of a president and other officers may be justified, but only on the understanding that they are to perform the tasks for which they are elected. Business meetings should be held quite apart from choir practices.

On no account should elected officers or committees be permitted to usurp the privileges of the choirmaster. They are not qualified to select music, for instance, and would be unable or unwilling to devote the necessary time to the task even if they had the qualifications. The music for the services, the choir practices, the personnel of the choir and the equipment are the choirmaster's responsibilities: therefore, while he may listen to and sometimes act upon suggestions from the choristers, decisions regarding the work of the choir must be his.

But there are duties which can and should be performed by voluntary assistants. Since these helpers must work well with the choirmaster, it would be better if they were appointed by him; but even if all the other offices are elective, the choirmaster should reserve the privilege of appointing his librarian.

A Secretary may relieve the choirmaster of the tasks of keeping attendance records and preparing service lists. If copies of all service lists are preserved they will be useful for reference and, with the attendance record, form a history of the choir's work and progress.

Apart from ordering music, there will be little correspondence, but what there is can be attended to by the secretary.

A Treasurer will be necessary only when the choir handles its own finances. He or she will receive contributions, issue checks on the authority of the choirmaster, and prepare a financial statement for presentation at the annual vestry meeting.

A Librarian who is faithful and knows his duties is a treasure. He should distribute and collect the music before and after services and at practices, keep the library and catalogue in good condition, repair books and sheet music, and report shortages or neglect to the choirmaster.

It is a good plan to give the librarian a list of music needed for each practice so that he may have it in readiness. If one anthem or service is distributed at a time there will be no confusion. An empty chair may be placed at each end of each row: the librarian can place sufficient copies of the next anthem at one end of the row ready to be passed along by the choristers, and as each anthem is finished it may be passed to the opposite end for collection.

Before services, the necessary music must be distributed among the choir stalls. When performing this duty, the librarian should wear his cassock even though he may be the only person in the church.

As he collects the music, the librarian will note any torn copies and lay them aside to be repaired before being returned to the library. He will also count the copies to make sure that none are missing. No chorister should take music away from the church without notifying the librarian.

Hymn books, psalters and chant books should be cared for by their users. However, if repairs have to be made, the librarian should make them. Since he will not handle the books as part of his routine work, he should be notified when repairs are necessary. A good plan is to have a list headed "Book Repairs" on which may be noted anything that requires the librarian's attention, such as the following:

7 Hymn Book—page 327 torn
16 Psalter—page 27 missing
11 Hymn Book—Binding ripped

Carelessness in handling books and music should not be dealt with by the librarian, but should be reported to the choirmaster who is the only person with the authority to take a chorister to task.

The librarian should be a permanent appointee since his efficiency will depend upon his familiarity with the library and his duties. An intelligent boy whose voice has changed, and who is reluctant to sever his connection with the choir, may make a good librarian; and when the time comes for him to take his place among the tenors or basses, he will be on hand to teach his successor.

Assistant librarians (and in some choirs they are needed) may be permanent, or the older choirboys may serve in rotation. Boys like to be given responsibilities, and it is a good thing to have one or two at a time working with the librarian.

The care of the vestments is an important duty that may be undertaken by some of the women of the church. If the members of the Chancel Guild can be persuaded to take over this work, one can be confident that it is in capable and experienced hands. Choristers should be urged to take good care of their vestments, not only in the interests of economy but also to make lighter the task of those who keep them in repair.

One member of the choir should be familiar with the vestments, and to him or her may be reported defects that require attention. This person should be the custodian of spare vestments and responsible for fitting out visitors or new choristers.

Some choirs which include boys have "choir mothers"—willing, patient women who see that the boys are properly vested, brushed and cleaned before going into service. Choir mothers are most helpful from an adult point of view, but boys hate being robbed of their independence by someone who insists upon straightening their ruffs and combing their hair. On the whole, it is perhaps wiser to have one's boys slightly unkempt and happy than well-groomed and sulky.

VI · CHOIR ETIQUETTE

Good manners and deportment in and around the church are of the utmost importance, and the behavior of the choristers must be a pattern for the whole congregation.

In parishes where the people have been taught from childhood to regard the church as the house of God, reverence and decorum will be natural reflections of the choir's spiritual approach to the services. In other places, where laxity and negligence have resulted in conduct that is hardly respectful, much less reverent (and, alas! there are such parishes) the choirmaster's insistence on reverent behavior will serve to remind the choir—and perhaps the congregation as well—of the nature of the church and the purpose of their presence there.

It is possible to overburden any organization with regulations, and the posting of a long list of rules is apt to have disappointing results. On the other hand, if it is explained to the choristers that certain conduct is prescribed for *their* benefit, and for the good of *their* group, they will probably respond with willingness.

Of certain ritualistic customs we shall say nothing: they vary in different parishes, and their observance is too much a matter of conscience and conviction to be dealt with here. However, there are certain standards of behavior that are considered necessary in all churches, Evangelical and Catholic alike; and choirs which fall below these standards are considered to be badly trained by their choirmasters and poorly instructed by their rectors.

The first rule for a chorister is that he be present at services and rehearsals. He can scarcely observe the other rules if he does not keep this one. He should honor his engagements with the church, the choirmaster and his fellow-choristers as scrupulously as he would honor any other engagement. He would not be a member of the choir if his services were not important; and when he is absent, he throws an extra burden on the others. If he *must* be absent, common courtesy demands that he notify the choirmaster in advance, and he should not ask to be excused often. A chorister will sometimes excuse himself for neglect on the grounds that his services are voluntary. He should be disabused. For right-thinking people, voluntary service carries with it not extra privileges, but extra responsibilities.

The chorister should be punctual. If he has missed part of a practice he will be unprepared for part of the Sunday service, unless the choirmaster inconveniences the whole choir by repeating what the tardy member has missed.

Upon reaching the church for practice, the chorister will procure the necessary books from his rack and be prepared to take his place when the signal is given. He will sit where the choirmaster asks him to sit. Unseemly displays of temper have often resulted from asking a chorister to move from a seat he has long occupied. He must understand that the change is being made for a good reason, and not in order that one of the choirmaster's favorites may have his treasured seat.

During rehearsal, the chorister will give the choirmaster his undivided attention. There will probably be opportunities for exchange of remarks with one's neighbors—some choirs have a short recess during rehearsal—but conversation must cease as soon as the choirmaster asks for attention. All choristers should be encouraged to ask the choirmaster for extra help if they find passages unusually difficult.

Anthems should be handled with reasonable care, and properly folded before being passed down the row for collection by the librarian.

At the conclusion of the practice there should be a dismissal prayer by the rector or, if he is not present, by the choirmaster. The chorister should then return his books to their proper place rather than leave them for someone else to pick up.

If the rehearsal is in the church proper, more formality must be observed. The choristers should don their cassocks, the boys their ruffs, the women their caps, and remain in the choir vestry until the time for which practice has been called. On no account should the choristers be permitted to straggle into the church and indulge in conversation before the practice begins.

At the appointed hour, the choristers should form in procession and proceed to the chancel, where a prayer will be said. There must be no conversation among the choristers during practice. When the rehearsal is over, the dismissal prayer is said and the choristers file from the church in procession. Books and vestments are returned to the spaces provided for them.

In parishes where church training has been allowed to lapse, choristers sometimes express the opinion that such formality at rehearsals is "a lot of nonsense." It can be nonsense, of course, if the reason for it is not explained; but, once the explanation has been made, the choristers soon begin to realize the significance of their duties, and to feel a renewed respect and affection for the church.

The choristers should be in the choir vestry at least fifteen minutes before services, and don all their vestments except surplices. There can be no objection to conversation providing that it cannot be heard in the church, or to some freedom of movement. Five minutes before the service, a bell should be rung or some other signal given for putting on surplices. Conversation should then cease, for the choristers are on duty from the moment they are surpliced. (No surpliced chorister should leave the choir vestry until he enters the church for the service.) The choristers then procure their books and service lists, and are seated in such an order that the procession is formed when they stand.

The choristers rise when the rector enters and, after the prayer, proceed to the chancel or to the place where the processional hymn is begun. The procession should be at a dignified pace, and each chorister should be at least his arm's length behind the chorister who precedes him.

It is not necessary to adopt a stiff or uncomfortable posture while standing, sitting or kneeling, but there should be no lounging or slouching. Choristers should not allow their eyes to wander to the nave: their duties are quite sufficient to occupy their whole attention. Needless to say, there should be no whispering or inattentiveness during the service.

At the conclusion of the service, a dismissal prayer is said in the choir vestry (not, properly, in the church) and after surplices have been removed, conversation may begin.

To the choirmaster who fears that such strict discipline may prove irksome to the choristers, let it be said that loyalty and enthusiasm are generally found in a well-disciplined choir, rarely in one that has no discipline at all.

The organist and choirmaster must at all times be a model for the choristers. He (or they) should never enter the church without a cassock, or be guilty of any levity or irreverence. If, after the service, the organist is approached by people who wish to speak to him about the music, it takes but an instant to slip off one's surplice before entering into a conversation.

CONCLUSION

Skill, zeal, understanding, loyalty to his choir, consideration for others—all these qualities are necessary for a successful organist and choirmaster. But they are not enough, for there will be times when discouragement, resentment and irritation will becloud one's judgement and threaten failure.

Man can accomplish no good work by his own efforts or for his own ends; and those whose work lies in the house of God should know what a practical thing it is to seek God's guidance and ask God's blessing upon their efforts.

It is a rare privilege to bring one's gifts to the altar week after week. Pray for inspiration, for guidance, for wisdom, and that the gifts may be worthy of acceptance. No sounder or more practical advice is contained in any book.

INDEX

Absolution:
  Holy Communion, 114
  Morning and Evening Prayer, 85, 100, 132, 133
Accession Service, 28, 130-131
Accompaniments, 5, 6, 7, 52, 53, 84, 85, 86, 90, 91, 92, 94, 95, 103, 108, 111, 113, 114, 115, 128, 135
Advent, 13, 14, 87, 91, 92, 101, 109
  1st Sunday in, 14, 25
  2nd Sunday in, 13, 14, 101, 109
  3rd Sunday in, 14, 92
  4th Sunday in, 14, 15, 25
Agnus Dei, 79, 105, 117, 118
Alleluias, 18, 20
All Saints' Day, 27, 116
Annunciation of the Blessed Virgin Mary, 25, 26, 87, 92, 101, 116
Anthems, 2, 6, 7, 9, 10, 12, 13, 14, 18, 19, 20, 21, 23, 68-71, 98, 102, 103, 105, 110, 111, 112, 121, 123, 128, 134, 137, 139, 156, 158
Anthems in place of Venite, 89, 96, 97, 107, 110, 126, 133
Antiphonal Singing, 52, 53, 90, 94
Antiphons: *see* Invitatories
Ascension Day, 8, 22, 26, 87, 89, 94, 107, 110, 111, 115
  Sunday after, 22
Ash Wednesday, 8, 19, 20, 25, 26, 89, 129

Banns of Marriage, 92, 111
Baptism, 92, 121-123
Benedic, anima mea, 101
Benedicite, 91, 92
Benediction, 98, 99, 102, 109, 120, 133, 139, 141
Benedictus, 92, 93
Benedictus es, 92
Benedictus qui venit, 79, 105, 116, 117, 118
Bible Sunday: *see* Advent, 2nd Sunday in
Bishops, Festivals of, 27
Blessed Virgin Mary: *see* Annunciation *and* Purification
Bonum est, 101
Books, 152, 156-158, 167, 168
Boys, Choir, 10, 11, 66, 154, 155, 168, 171
Burial of the Dead, 28, 127-129

Calendars, 12, 13, 27, 29-36
Cantate Domino (Isa. 42:10–12), 133
Cantate Domino (Psalm 98), 101
Canticles, 1, 6, 37-54, 80, 88, 89, 91, 92, 93, 100, 101, 102, 122, 123, 132, 133
Cantor, 53, 83, 84, 93, 103
Cantoris, 52, 53, 84, 90
Caps, Choir, 155, 171
Carol Service, 15, 165
Cassocks, 141, 142, 153, 154, 167, 171, 172
Chant Books, 37-54, 156, 157
Chanting, 4, 6, 37-54, 54-58, 80, 88, 89, 90, 91, 92, 93, 94, 101, 102, 103, 104, 129, 130, 132, 133, 134, 137, 139, 140
Chants, 4, 6, 37-54, 88, 89, 90, 91, 120, 130, 131, 156, 157
  Gregorian, 53, 54
Children's Service, 132
Choir Stalls, 152
Choristers, 3, 4, 8-11, 169-172
Christmas, 9, 14, 15, 16, 87, 92

Christmas Day, 8, 14, 15, 16, 25, 87, 89, 94, 107, 109, 110, 111, 115
1st Sunday after, 15, 101
2nd Sunday after, 16, 102
Circumcision of Christ, 16
Clergy, 1, 2, 3, 8, 76, 77, 78
Collars, 154, 155
Collects:
Holy Communion, 107
Morning and Evening Prayer, 80, 81, 95, 96, 102, 132
Proper, 12, 13, 14, 15, 16, 17, 18, 19, 20, 21, 22, 23, 24, 25, 26, 27, 28, 86, 89, 109, 110, 127, 129, 131, 133, 134, 137, 140, 141
Comfortable Words, 105, 114, 115, 116
Commination Service, 19, 129-130
Committees:
Choir, 165, 166
Music, 3
Communion Service (settings), 70, 105-121
Conferences, 76-78
Confession:
Ely, 85
Holy Communion, 113, 114
Morning and Evening Prayer, 84, 85, 95, 100, 132, 133
Confessors, Festivals of, 27
Confirmation, 28, 123-124
Consecration of a Church, 28, 139-141
Console, Organ, 151
Conventions, 28
Conversion of St. Paul: *see* Saints' Days: St. Paul
Cottas, 153
Creed:
Apostles', 93, 102, 111, 128, 131, 132, 133
Nicene, 93, 105, 111, 112, 123, 124
St. Athanasian, 93, 94
Cupboards, 157, 162, 163
Curate: *see* Clergy

Decalogue: *see* Ten Commandments
Decani, 52, 53, 83, 90
Descants, 10, 53, 66, 67, 90, 108, 157, 158
Deus misereatur, 101
Dominion Day, 28, 131

Easter, 9, 20-22, 26, 87
Easter Day, 17, 18, 20, 21, 23, 26, 89, 94, 107, 110, 111, 115
1st Sunday after, 21
2nd Sunday after, 21, 26
3rd Sunday after, 26
4th Sunday after, 26
5th Sunday after, 22, 26
Easter Even, 19, 20, 109
Ember Days, 14, 19, 20, 22, 23, 25
Epiphany, 16, 17, 23, 25, 87, 94, 115, 116
Epistles, 12, 13, 14, 15, 16, 17, 18, 19, 20, 21, 22, 23, 24, 25, 27, 28, 105, 109, 110, 127, 129, 131, 133, 134, 137, 141
Etiquette, 169-172
Eucharist: *see* Holy Communion
Evening Prayer, 55, 56, 57, 58, 100-102, 103, 123, 124, 129, 131, 132, 133, 134, 140, 142
Evensong: *see* Evening Prayer
Eves, 24, 25, 27. *See also various Saints' Days and other Holy Days*
Exhortation:
Holy Communion, 112, 113
Morning and Evening Prayer, 84, 99, 100, 133

Faux Bourdons, 65, 66, 67, 108, 157
Finances, 164-165
Funerals: *see* Burial of the Dead

Gloria in Excelsis, 100, 105, 120
Gloria Patri, 52, 53, 88, 89, 91, 92, 93, 94, 100, 101, 126, 128, 133, 137
Gloria Tibi, 105, 110
Good Friday, 8, 20, 89, 107, 110
Gospels, 12, 13, 14, 15, 16, 17, 18, 19, 20, 21, 22, 23, 24, 25, 27, 28, 92, 93, 101, 102, 105, 109, 110, 111, 121, 123, 124, 127, 129, 131, 133, 134, 137, 141

Gradual, 110
Gratias Tibi, 111, 123
Gregorian Chants, 53, 54

Harvest Thanksgiving, 28, 133-134
Holy Communion, 21, 22, 28, 79, 103, 104, 105-121, 123, 124, 127, 129, 131, 134, 137, 140, 141
Holy Days, 12, 21, 23-27, 87. *See also various Saints' Days and other Holy Days*
  Transference of, 15, 24, 25, 26, 27
Holy Innocents: *see* Innocents' Day
Holy Week, 20, 26. *See also* Easter Even, Good Friday
Hymn Books, 156, 157, 158
Hymns, 1, 2, 4, 5, 6, 12, 13, 14, 15, 16, 17, 18, 19, 20, 21, 22, 23, 24, 25, 58-68, 74, 75, 80, 81, 82, 83, 96, 97, 98, 99, 100, 102, 103, 104, 105, 107, 110, 111, 112, 118, 119, 121, 122, 123, 124, 125, 126, 127, 128, 129, 131, 132, 133, 134, 135, 136, 137, 139, 140, 142
  For Children, 16
  Metres, 60, 61
  Missionary, 17, 25
  Phrasing, 62, 63, 64, 65, 119
  Processional, 67, 81, 82, 105, 123, 125, 171
  Recessional, 99, 127
  Tunes, 1, 59, 60, 61, 65

Improvisation, 7, 73, 94, 96, 98, 103, 104, 106, 112, 115, 118, 125, 126, 128, 130, 140. *See also* Accompaniments, Modulation
Independence Day, 28
Inductions, 28, 134-137
Innocents' Day, 15, 16, 25
Institutions, 28, 134-137
Intoning, 3, 54-58, 80, 81, 82, 83, 84, 85, 86, 93, 94, 95, 96, 97, 98, 99, 103, 104, 105, 106, 107, 108, 109, 111, 112, 113, 114, 115, 117, 118, 120, 122, 124, 126, 128, 129, 130, 131, 132, 133, 135, 137, 139, 140. *See also* Responses
Introit, 106, 107
Invitation (Holy Communion), 113, 114
Invitatories, 86, 87, 88, 89

Jubilate Deo, 37, 93, 132, 139

Kneeling Benches, 152
Kyrie, 105, 108, 109

Laus Tibi, 111, 123
Laying of a Foundation Stone, 138-139
Lectionaries, 12, 13, 14, 15, 19, 20, 24, 92, 101, 102. *See also* Lessons
Lent, 18, 19, 20, 25, 26, 91, 109
  1st Sunday in, 19, 109
  3rd Sunday in, 26
  4th Sunday in, 20, 26
  5th Sunday in, 20, 26
  6th Sunday in, 19, 20, 26
  See also Ash Wednesday, Easter Even, Good Friday, Holy Week
Lessons, 2, 12, 13, 14, 16, 17, 18, 19, 22, 23, 24, 27, 86, 91, 92, 100, 101, 121, 128, 131, 132, 133, 134, 139. *See also* Lectionaries
Librarian, 162, 163, 167, 168, 170
Library, 162, 163
Litany, 52, 102-104, 129, 131
"Little Lent," 17, 18, 91
Lord's Prayer:
  Holy Communion, 105, 107, 117, 120
  Morning and Evening Prayer, 80, 81, 85, 86, 95, 100, 102, 131, 133, 135

Magnificat, 101
Martyrs, Festivals of, 27
Mass: *see* Holy Communion
Matrimony, 28, 124-127
Matrons, Festivals of, 27
Mattins: *see* Morning Prayer
Merit Badges, 155, 156
Miserere, mei Deus, 130
Missions, Service for, 28, 132-133

Modulation, 7, 82, 83, 88, 90, 96, 97, 99, 103, 104, 106, 107, 111, 112, 120, 128. *See also* Improvisation
Morning Prayer, 55, 56, 57, 58, 80-100, 103, 121, 122, 123, 124, 129, 131, 132, 133, 134, 140
Mothering Sunday, 20
Music Committees, 3

Nativity of our Lord: *see* Christmas Day
Nativity of St. John the Baptist: *see* Saints' Days: St. John the Baptist
New Year's Day: *see* Circumcision of Christ
Numbered Equipment, 157, 162
Nunc Dimittis, 101, 102, 121, 128

Offertory, 98, 102, 109, 112, 115, 133
Offertory Sentence, 98, 102, 112
Ordinations, 27, 28
Organ, 144-151
Organization, 165-168
Organ Music, 5, 6, 71-74, 98, 99, 112, 118, 119, 120, 121, 122, 123, 125, 126, 127, 128, 141, 142. *See also* Accompaniments, Improvisation, Modulation, Organ Prelude
Organ Prelude, 72, 73, 81, 100, 106, 140
Organ Recitals, 141-143
Organ Voluntary: *see* Organ Prelude

Palm Sunday, 19, 20, 26
Passion Sunday, 20, 26
Pater Noster: *see* Lord's Prayer
Patronal Festivals, 27
Penitential Office, 19, 129-130
Piano, 138, 139, 163
Plainsong, 53, 54, 59, 119
Pointing, 6, 37-51
Practices, Choir: *see* Rehearsals
Practices, Congregational, 74
Prayer Books, 156
Precentor: *see* Cantor
Prefaces (Holy Communion), 105, 115, 116
Pre-Lenten Season, 17, 18, 91
Presentation of Christ in the Temple: *see* Purification of the Blessed Virgin Mary
Psalms, 1, 2, 6, 12, 14, 24, 37-54, 80, 88, 89, 90, 91, 100, 110, 126, 127, 128, 129, 130, 131, 132, 133, 134, 137, 139, 140, 156, 157
Psalters, 4, 37-54, 156, 157, 158
Purification of the Blessed Virgin Mary, 25, 87, 102, 116, 121

Quadragesima, 19
Quicumque vult, 93, 94
Quinquagesima, 18, 25

Rector: *see* Clergy
Rehearsals, 9, 163, 164, 166, 169, 170, 171
Responses, 54-58, 80, 86, 94, 95, 100, 102, 109, 124, 126, 130, 131, 132, 133, 135, 137, 138, 139
Rogation Days, 22, 26, 103
Rogation Sunday, 22, 26
Ruffs, 154, 155, 171

Saints' Days:
- St. Andrew, 25, 94
- St. Barnabas, 26, 27
- St. Bartholomew, 27, 94
- St. James, 27, 94
- St. John the Baptist, 27, 93, 94
- St. John the Evangelist, 15, 16, 25
- St. Luke, 27
- St. Mark, 26
- St. Mary: *see* Annunciation *and* Purification
- St. Matthew, 27, 94
- St. Matthias, 25, 94
- St. Michael and All Angels, 27
- St. Paul, Conversion of, 25
- St. Peter, 27
- St. Philip and St. James, 26
- St. Simon and St. Jude, 27, 94, 134, 137

Saints' Days (*continued*)
St. Stephen, 15, 16, 25
St. Thomas, 21, 25
See also All Saints' Day
Sanctus, 105, 115, 116, 117, 118
Select Vestry, 3
Sentences:
Burial, 127, 128
Morning and Evening Prayer, 82, 83, 86, 100, 132, 133
Septuagesima, 18, 25
Service Lists, 97, 158-162, 165
Service of Praise, 141-143
Sexagesima, 18, 25
Sight Reading, 10
Social Service, 28
Solos, 9, 71, 72, 126, 142
Summary of the Law, 108, 109
Sunday Schools, 58, 75, 76, 132
Surge Illuminator, 133
Surplices, 141, 142, 153, 154, 171, 172
Sursum Corda, 105, 114, 115, 116

Tables, Prayer Book, 12, 13, 14, 17, 19, 20, 24, 79, 89
Te Deum, 37, 51, 70, 91, 131
Ten Commandments, 107, 108, 109
Thanksgiving Day, 28, 89, 107, 110
Thanksgiving, General, 97, 140
Thanksgiving, Harvest; *see* Harvest Thanksgiving
Transfiguration of our Lord, 27, 87, 116
Trinity, Season of, 23, 27, 92, 101, 102
Trinity Sunday, 23, 27, 87, 94, 111, 115

Unison Singing, 10, 52, 53, 65, 67, 70, 90, 91, 94

Venite, 37, 52, 88, 89, 133
Versicles: *see* Responses
Vestments, 141, 142, 153-156, 162, 167, 168, 171, 172
Vestry, 162-163
Vigils: *see* Eves
Virgins, Festivals of, 27

Wardens, 3, 164
Watch-Night Service, 16
Weddings: *see* Matrimony
Whit Sunday, 22, 27, 87, 89, 92, 94, 107, 110, 111, 115
Whitsuntide, 22, 23, 27